CW01072506

The **AA** POCKET

NEW
ZEALAND

New Zealand: Regions and Best places to see

 Best places to see 24–45

 Featured sight

 Upper North Island 49–73

 Upper South Island 90–107

 Lower North Island 74–89

 Lower South Island 108–129

Original text by Allan Edie
Updated by Susi Bailey

© Automobile Association Developments Limited 2008. First published 2008

ISBN: 978-0-7495-5761-4

Published by AA Publishing, a trading name of Automobile Association Developments
Limited, whose registered office is Fanum House, Basing View, Basingstoke,
Hampshire RG21 4EA. Registered number 1878835.

Colour separation: Keenes, Andover
Printed and bound in Italy by Printer Trento S.r.l.

Front cover images: (t) AA/P Kenward; (b) AA/M Langford
Back cover image: AA/A Reisinger & V Meduna

A03604
Maps in this title produced from map data © New Holland Publishing (South Africa)
(PTY) Limited 2007

About this book

This book is divided into four sections:

Planning pages 10–23
Before you go; Getting there; Getting around; Being there

Best places to see pages 24–45
The unmissable highlights of any visit to New Zealand

Exploring pages 46–129
The best places to visit in New Zealand, organized by area

Maps pages 133–144
All map references are to the maps in the atlas. For example, Christchurch has the reference ✚ 135 E7 – indicating the page number and grid square in which it can be found

Contents

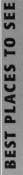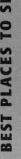

Planning

Before you go

WHEN TO GO

JAN	FEB	MAR	APR	MAY	JUN	JUL	AUG	SEP	OCT	NOV	DEC
23°C	23°C	22°C	20°C	18°C	15°C	13°C	14°C	16°C	18°C	19°C	22°C
73°F	73°F	72°F	68°F	64°F	59°F	55°F	57°F	61°F	64°F	66°F	72°F

🔲 High season 🔲 Low season

New Zealand's summer lasts from December through February, although November and March can also be hot. The peak period for visitors is summer, which is when many festivals are held and most Kiwis also take their annual holiday. As a result, accommodations and sights tend to be busy. The winter ski season (Jun–Sep) attracts visitors to resorts on Mount Ruapehu and in the Southern Alps.

WHAT YOU NEED

● Required
○ Suggested
▲ Not required

Some countries require a passport to remain valid for a minimum period (usually at least six months) beyond the date of entry – check before you travel.

	UK	Germany	USA	Canada	Australia	Ireland	Netherlands	Spain
Passport (or National Identity Card where applicable)	●	●	●	●	●	●	●	●
Visa (regulations can change – check before you travel)	▲	▲	▲	▲	▲	▲	▲	▲
Onward or Return Ticket	●	●	●	●	●	●	●	●
Health Inoculations	▲	▲	▲	▲	▲	▲	▲	▲
Health Documentation (▶ 13, Health Insurance)	○	○	○	○	○	○	○	○
Travel Insurance	○	○	○	○	○	○	○	○
Driving Licence (national)	●	●	●	●	●	●	●	●
Car Insurance Certificate	▲	▲	▲	▲	▲	▲	▲	▲
Car Registration Document	▲	▲	▲	▲	▲	▲	▲	▲

WEBSITES

● www.aatravel.co.nz
Visitor information site of New Zealand Automobile Association.

● www.destination-nz.com
Online travel guide, with accommodations and sights.

- www.doc.govt.nz
  Department of Conservation
  website, with information on
  national and other parks.

- www.newzealand.com
  Official website of Tourism
  New Zealand.

- www.i-site.org
  Lists Tourism New Zealand's
  visitor centres around the
  country.

- www.tourism.net.nz
  Lists over 12,000 New Zealand
  tourism and travel sites.

TOURIST OFFICES AT HOME

In the UK
Tourism New Zealand
New Zealand House
80 Haymarket
London
SW1Y 4QT
☎ 020 7930 1662;
www.newzealand.com

In the USA
Tourism New Zealand
Suite 2510
222 East 41st Street
New York
NY10017
☎ 212/661-7088;
www.newzealand.com

HEALTH INSURANCE
Some emergency medical services are subsidized for visitors from
Australia and the UK, but all visitors are strongly recommended to arrange
medical insurance coverage before their trip.

TIME DIFFERENCES

| GMT 12 noon | New Zealand 12 midnight | Germany 1PM | USA (NY) 7AM | Netherlands 1PM | Spain 1PM |

New Zealand standard time is 12 hours ahead of Greenwich Mean Time
(GMT+12). New Zealand's proximity to the International Date Line makes
it one of the first countries to see each new day.

NATIONAL HOLIDAYS

1–2 Jan *New Year*
6 Feb *Waitangi Day*
Mar/Apr *Good Friday*
Mar/Apr *Easter Monday*
25 Apr *ANZAC Day*
Jun (first Mon) *Queen's Birthday*
Oct (fourth Mon) *Labour Day*
25 Dec *Christmas Day*
26 Dec *Boxing Day*

Most stores and attractions are closed on Christmas Day, Good Friday and the morning of Anzac Day. Tourist amenities are usually open on the other public holidays.

You will also find that there are regional holidays during the year, corresponding to the founding days of each of the country's 13 provinces. The main ones are:
Wellington region: third Monday in January.
Auckland, Bay of Islands, Rotorua and Taupo: last Monday in January.
Christchurch: during Cup and Show Week in November.
Queenstown and Dunedin: last Monday in March.

WHAT'S ON WHEN

January *Yachting Regatta,* Auckland: the world's largest one-day sailing regatta is held on Auckland harbour (last Monday in January).
World Buskers Festival, Christchurch: features international acts.

February *Wine Marlborough Festival* Blenheim, Marlborough (second or third weekend of February).

February/March *International Arts Festival,* Wellington (biennial, in even years).

March *Wild Foods Festival,* Hokitika.
Golden Shears sheep-shearing competition, Masterton.

Easter *Royal Easter Show,* Auckland.

April *Warbirds over Wanaka,* Wanaka: the largest aviation show in the southern hemisphere (biennial, in odd years).

June *National Agricultural Fieldays,* Hamilton: one of the world's largest agricultural shows, held over four days at Mystery Creek (second week of the month).

July *Winter Festival,* Queenstown: a ten-day festival marking the start of the ski season.

September *Blossom Festival,* Alexandra.
World of Wearable Art Festival, Wellington.

October *Taranaki Rhododendron and Garden Festival,* New Plymouth: takes place over two weeks.

November *Ellerslie Flower Show,* Auckland: held over five days (second week).
Cup and Show Week, Christchurch (mid-November).
Guy Fawkes evening, countrywide: fireworks on 5 November.

Getting there

BY AIR

Auckland (North Island)

23km (14 miles) to city centre

- N/A
- 40 minutes
- 30 minutes

Christchurch (South Island)

11km (7 miles) to city centre

- N/A
- 30 minutes
- 20 minutes

Most visitors arrive by air, through the three main international airports of Auckland, Wellington and Christchurch. Auckland Airport (☎ 09 256 8899; www.auckland-airport.co.nz) is the country's largest gateway. Airbuses operate from the international terminal every 20 minutes during the day and half-hourly in the evening Nov–Apr daily 4:40am–10pm; May–Oct daily 6:20am–10pm. The domestic terminals, serving Air New Zealand and Qantas, are a 10-minute walk from the international terminal; a free shuttle bus connects them running every 20 minutes daily 6am–10:30pm, or follow the blue line on the pavement.

Wellington Airport (☎ 04 385 5100; www.wlg-airport.co.nz) mainly handles flights from New Zealand and Australian destinations and is 10km (6 miles) from the city. Stagecoach Flyer buses connect the terminal with downtown stops half-hourly Mon–Fri 6:20am–8:20pm, and half-hourly or hourly Sat–Sun 6:50am–8:50pm.

Christchurch Airport (☎ 03 358 5029; www.christchurch-airport.co.nz) is 11km (9 miles) from the city. The Red Bus City Flyer operates between the terminal and the city half-hourly or hourly Mon–Fri 6:35am–12:55am, Sat 8:10am–12:55am, Sun 8:40am–12:55am.

The national airline is Air New Zealand (☎ 0800 737000; www.airnz.co.nz). It flies between New Zealand and the UK, Australia, USA and various Pacific and Asian destinations, and in addition connects all major centres within the country via a domestic network. There are also several smaller air services operating short hops and scenic flights.

Getting around

PUBLIC TRANSPORT

Regional flights Air New Zealand and Qantas fly the principal routes in the country and link about 30 destinations. Both offer air passes which must be bought before travelling to New Zealand but can be open-dated.

Trains TranzScenic (☎ 04 495 0775; www.tranzscenic.co.nz) operates three main rail routes: the Overlander from Auckland to Wellington; the TranzCoastal from Picton to Christchurch; and the TranzAlpine from Christchurch to Greymouth (➤ 40–41). Various travel passes are available, which allow travel on rail routes and the Interislander ferry, and on InterCity long-distance bus lines.

Coaches and buses The InterCity long-distance bus network (www.intercitycoach.co.nz) covers much of the country. Newmans (www.newmanscoach.co.nz) operates all major routes and some companies offer tours by long-distance bus.

Ferries The main inter-island ferry service is operated by TranzRail (☎ 04 498 3302). It is a roll-on roll-off service carrying passengers, motor vehicles and railroad wagons. There are several round-trip sailings from Wellington to Picton each day, taking 3 hours each way.

Urban transport Christchurch has an upgraded heritage tramway system and Auckland has a good bus network. Wellington is a major transport centre and ferry terminal, with a cable car from downtown to the upper slopes of the Kelburn area. Bicyclists are also well provided for.

FARES AND TICKETS

TranzScenic, InterCity and Newmans all have travel passes that allow you to save a lot of money if you plan to stick to rail and bus networks, and some also include inter-island ferry services. Senior citizens, young people and students are eligible for discounts with these companies.

TAXIS

Taxis can be rented from stands; they can also be flagged down. In some towns taxis even offer a rate that is lower than a bus service. For long-distance journeys negotiate the fare in advance. You are not expected to tip taxi drivers.

DRIVING

- Speed limits on motorways: 100kph (62mph)
  Speed limits on main roads: 100kph (62mph)
  Speed limits on urban roads: 50kph (31mph)
- Vehicles drive on the left, and seatbelts must be worn in all seats where fitted at all times.
- Random breath and blood testing. Limit: 80mg (0.08g of alcohol in 100ml of blood. For drivers under 20 the limit is 30mg (0.03g) in 100ml.

- Petrol (fuel) comes in two grades: unleaded 96 octane and unleaded 91 octane. Diesel and LPG (liquefied petroleum gas) are also available. In rural areas service stations may be scarce and may be closed on weekends or outside normal hours. Major towns and cities have 24-hour stations.
- There are plenty of garages and service stations throughout the country and most rental companies include free roadside assistance as part of the rental package. Automobile Association members receive free reciprocal membership of the New Zealand AA, including roadside assistance, maps and accommodations guides (☎ 09 377 4660; www.nzaa.co.nz).

CAR RENTAL

All the major rental firms are represented in New Zealand. You must be at least 21 to rent a car or motor home. For inter-island travel, many companies require you to leave the vehicle on one island and pick up another after leaving the ferry. One-way rentals can also be arranged.

Being there

TOURIST OFFICES

Auckland
SkyCity, corner of Victoria
and Federal streets
☎ 09 367 6009;
www.aucklandnz.com

Wellington
Civic Square, corner of Victoria and
Wakefield streets
☎ 04 802 4860;
www.wellingtonnz.com

Christchurch
Old Chief Post Office
Cathedral Square
☎ 03 379 9629;
www.christchurchinformation.co.nz

Queenstown
Clocktower Building, corner of
Shotover and Camp streets
☎ 03 442 4100;
www.queenstown-vacation.com

Around 100 regional and local
tourist offices throughout the
country form the Visitor Information
Network, co-ordinated by Tourism
New Zealand. Because they are
linked in one network, Visitor
Information Centres, known as
i-SITES, can access information
on other areas. They provide an
invaluable, up-to-date service and
should be your first port of call.

MONEY
New Zealand currency is decimal based and
divided into dollars and cents. The New Zealand
dollar is not tied to any other currency. Coins
that are now in circulation are in denominations
of 10, 20 and 50 cents, and 1 and 2 dollars.
Notes are in denominations of 5, 10, 20, 50
and 100 dollars.

There is no limit to the amount of New
Zealand dollars that may be brought into or
taken out of the country.

Credit cards are widely accepted and include
Mastercard, Visa, American Express and Diners Club, and travellers'
cheques can be changed at banks or change bureaux in all towns.

TIPS/GRATUITIES

Tipping is not generally expected, but may be given to reward excellent service

Yes ✓   No ✗

Hotels (if service included)	✗
Restaurants (if service not included)	✗
Cafés/bars (if service not included)	✗
Taxis	✗
Tour guides	✗
Porters/ Chambermaids	✗
Toilet attendants	✗

POSTAL AND INTERNET SERVICES

The logo for NZ Post Limited is a stylized envelope. There are two levels of post for letters and parcels nationwide: Standard Post (2–3-day delivery) and FastPost (next-day delivery). Post offices are open Mon–Fri 9–5pm.

Most hotels provide in-room Internet access. There are also Internet cafés in most areas and public libraries with Internet.

TELEPHONES

Telecom operates the public telephone service and most call boxes use Telecom phone cards, available from shops. For directory enquiries dial 018, and for international directory enquiries dial 0172. The country code for New Zealand is 64.

International dialling codes

Australia: 00 61
Germany: 00 49
Hong Kong: 00 852
Malaysia: 00 60
Singapore: 00 65
UK: 00 44
USA and Canada: 00 1

Emergency telephone number

Police, Fire, Ambulance: 111

EMBASSIES AND CONSULATES

UK ☎ 04 924 2888
Germany ☎ 04 473 6063
USA ☎ 04 462 6000
Netherlands ☎ 04 471 6390
Canada ☎ 04 473 9577

HEALTH ADVICE

The most serious potential health risk in New Zealand is from the sun. Ultra-violet radiation throughout the country is particularly high. Take adequate precautions, even on overcast days, by wearing a sun hat and using a sunscreen with a high protection factor. Always ensure that children are well protected.

Drugs Pharmacies are usually open during normal shopping hours. If you are on unusual medication, take supplies with you as there is no guarantee that they will be available locally. Take your prescription certificate to avoid difficulties with customs.

Safe water Tap water everywhere in New Zealand is safe to drink. City water supplies are chlorinated and most are also fluoridated. If camping in remote areas, always boil water before drinking.

PERSONAL SAFETY

There is an efficient police force modelled on the British system. Police do not carry arms. While New Zealand is generally a safe society, the usual sensible precautions should be taken to ensure personal safety:

● Avoid walking alone in dark areas of towns.
● If walking in bush or mountain country, take good maps, dress sensibly, take supplies of food and drink, and tell someone what your plans are.
● Beware of pickpockets.
● Do not leave valuables in unattended cars.

ELECTRICITY

The power supply in New Zealand is 230–240 volts AC. Sockets accept two- or three-flat-pin plugs. Hotels and motels provide 110-volt/20 watt AC sockets for shavers only. An adaptor will be required for those appliances that do not operate on 230 volts.

OPENING HOURS

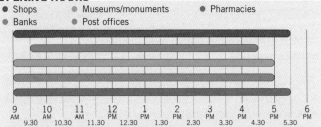

- ● Shops
- ● Banks
- ● Museums/monuments
- ● Post offices
- ● Pharmacies

In addition to the above, pharmacies and stores are open on Saturday 9–noon or 9–4 and some shops are open on Sunday. The bigger towns usually have late-night shopping on Thursday or Friday until 8:30 or 9pm. Some smaller shops close at lunchtime on Saturdays. Local convenience stores (dairies) are usually open 7am–8pm seven days a week.

Times of museum openings vary and many are open on weekends, too – for details see individual museums listed in the Exploring section of this guide.

LANGUAGE

The common language of New Zealand is English. The written language follows British spelling convention, rather than American. There is little difference in pronunciation from one part of the country to another, except that in the south of the South Island you may detect a Scottish accent. The Maori language is undergoing a revival; you will hear it spoken on a *marae* (the area surrounding a meeting house) and on some radio stations. Visitors may also hear Maori spoken on TV and radio, used as a greeting (*kia ora*), and in place names. The language was entirely oral until early missionaries recorded it in written form. The easiest way to say Maori words is to pronounce each syllable phonetically. 'Kiwi' English also tends to have its own idiosyncratic expressions or phrases.

COMMON MAORI WORDS AND PHRASES

ao cloud
Aotearoa Land of the Long White Cloud
ara path
atua god
awa river
haere mai welcome
haera ra farewell
hangi a Maori feast
hau wind
Hawaiki legendary homeland of the Maori
kia ora your good health
kumara a sweet potato
makomako bellbird
ma stream
mana prestige
manu bird
maunga mountain
moana sea or lake
moko tattoo
motu island, or anything that is isolated
pa fortified village
Pakeha foreigner, white person, European
po night
puke hill
puna spring (of water)
rangi sky
roto lake
rua two, eg Rotorua two lakes
tapu sacred
utu retribution
wai water
whanga bay, stretch of water, inlet
whare house
whenua land

'KIWI' ENGLISH

Aussie Australian
bach a holiday chalet (pronounced 'batch')
Beehive the main government building in Wellington
bludge scrounge, borrow
bush the forest
chook chicken
cocky farmer (usually cow-cocky)
chilly-bin portable cooler box
crib the South Island equivalent of a bach
crook sick, ill
dag a character, or entertaining person
dairy general store
gidday good day (hello)
good as gold fine, okay
handle beer glass with a handle
jandals flip-flops, thongs
judder bars speed bumps in the road
morning tea mid-morning tea or coffee break
mozzie mosquito
Pakeha person of European descent
Pom an English person (mildly derogatory)
smoko tea or coffee break
togs swimwear
wopwops the back of beyond

Best places to see

1 Fiordland National Park

www.fiordland.org.nz

Fiordland National Park is not only the largest national park in New Zealand, but one of the largest in the world.

In contrast to the coast at the north of the South Island, where the Marlborough Sounds offer a gentle landscape of bush-clad hills and meandering sea passages, the sounds of Fiordland National Park in the south are rugged, glacier-carved fjords with deep waters and precipitous sides. Inland is an unspoiled region of hills, deep lakes and mountains covering 12,500sq km (4,800sq miles), where rare species of wildlife have survived undisturbed. The high annual rainfall produces dramatic waterfalls. The most northerly of the fjords is Milford Sound, and the road leading there is one of the scenic highlights of New Zealand. You can also fly to Milford, or walk the Milford Track (➤ 126) over four days. Most of the other fjords are inaccessible other than by sea. A boat trip on Milford Sound is recommended; tours last two hours to two days. Sheer cliffs rising 1,200m (4,000ft) out of the water provide awesome photographic opportunities, while some tours include a visit to Milford Deep Underwater Observatory for a glimpse of the unique ecology of the fjords. The trip to Doubtful Sound via Lake Manapouri (➤ 122) and the Wilmot Pass is also a must. Cruises of up to a week can be taken to some of the sounds. The gateway to

Fiordland National Park is the township of Te Anau (➤ 127), on the shores of Lake Te Anau (the South Island's largest lake).

✚ 140 D2 ✉ Access to Milford Sound via SH94, north of Te Anau ⏰ Snow chains may be required in winter (☎ 0900 33 222) ✋ Free access 🍴 Blue Duck Bar and Café ($$), Milford Sound (☎ 03 249 7931) 🚌 Tours from Te Anau and Queenstown; www.realjourneys.co.nz; www.redboats.co.nz 🚢 Milford Sound: daily launches ✈ Flights from Queenstown, Wanaka and Te Anau
🛈 Lakefront Drive, Te Anau ☎ 03 249 8900; National park visitor centre ☎ 03 249 7924; www.doc.gov.nz

2 Tongariro National Park

This sacred 'land of fire', given by Maori to the New Zealand people in 1887, is now a UNESCO World Heritage Area.

Lying at the middle of the North Island's volcanic plateau is the island's highest mountain – the active volcanic peak of Mount Ruapehu (2,797m/9,176ft). Adjacent to it are Mount Ngauruhoe (2,291m/7,516 ft) and Mount Tongariro (1,968m/6,457ft), the trio forming the heart of a high and sometimes bleak area known as Tongariro National Park. The land was given to the government by the Maori tribal owners in 1887, when it became New Zealand's first – and the world's fourth – national park.

Tongariro is now New Zealand's most popular national park, mainly because of its excellent ski areas. The Whakapapa ski field lies on the northern slopes of Mount Ruapehu (20km/12 miles from the small community of National Park), and the Turoa field is on the southwestern slopes (served by the town of Ohakune). The ski season generally runs

from about late June to September – although sometimes it can run even longer.

Ruapehu is an active volcano with a warm crater lake and, although normally placid, there were eruptions in 1995 and 1996 and it is monitored constantly.

Cone-shaped Ngauruhoe periodically emits a cloud of steam, but rarely erupts. Tongariro is dormant, but has a hot spring on its slopes.

There are pleasant walking trails through the park, including the Tongariro Crossing, a full-day trek across the shoulders of Mount Tongariro. For those who are fit enough, it is possible to make a side trip to the top of Tongariro, or even to Ngauruhoe.

➕ 136 C4 ✉ Whakapapa is the end of SH48, off SH47 between SH1 and SH4 🕔 All year (roads may close due to to winter snow) ✋ Free access 🍴 Chateau Tongariro ($$$) at Whakapapa 🚌 National Park and Ohakune 🚉 National Park and Ohakune stations

🛈 Whakapapa Village, Mount Ruapehu ☎ 07 892 3729; www.whakapapa.co.nz

3 Te Papa Tongarewa

www.tepapa.govt.nz

Bold, imaginative, constantly changing and always fun, Te Papa is New Zealand's leading-edge national museum.

Te Papa is a bicultural museum and has a variety of exhibitions that tell the stories, and display the *taonga* (treasures), of the Maori people, the *tangata whenua*, or first settlers of New Zealand.

Hands-on exhibitions such as Awesome Forces and Mountains to Sea describe the formation of the land, and the creatures that live on it, while Bush City brings the natural world into the middle of the capital.

The stories of New Zealand's immigrants are dramatically conveyed in Passports, while Made in New Zealand looks at 300 years of Maori and Pakeha art and visual culture. Golden Days is where you can see 100 years of New Zealand history come alive in just 12 minutes!

For those who enjoy a bit of a thrill, the Time Warp will delight, It includes Blastback and Future Rush – exciting time-travel rides. For children there are Discovery Centres, with plenty of touchy-feely activities, plus StoryPlace for the very young.

✚ 144 E4 ✉ Cable Street, Wellington ☎ 04 381 7000 🕐 Fri–Wed 10–6; Thu 10–9 💷 General admission to Te Papa and most exhibitions free; charges (inexpensive) for some special exhibitions, Time Warp and guided tours 🍴 Te Papa Café ($); Espresso café ($)

4 Whakarewarewa Thermal Reserve

If you have time to see only one attraction in the Rotorua region, then 'Whaka' (as the reserve is commonly known) should be it.

The city of Rotorua (➤ 66), near the middle of the North Island, is renowned for volcanic activity, evidenced by spouting geysers, bubbling mud and a pervasive smell of hydrogen sulphide.

About 3km (2 miles) from the heart of the city, Whakarewarewa is the most famous of Rotorua's five thermal areas. The reserve is split into two areas. The main one, **Te Puia,** contains the Pohutu (Maori for 'splashing') geyser, which spouts up 30m (100ft) at regular intervals, and the smaller Prince of Wales Feathers geyser (12m/40ft), which always erupts first. Nearby are cauldrons of bubbling mud and moonscape-like silica formations.

Te Puia is also home to the New Zealand Maori Arts and Crafts Institute, established in the 1960s to promote Maori crafts. There's also a shop and kiwi house, and a concert of Maori songs and dance presented daily at 12:15, 3:15 and 6:15 (5:15 in winter).

The rest of the thermal reserve is taken up by **Whakarewarewa Thermal Village,** a living Maori village whose occupants escort tours, perform cultural shows and dish up *hangi* meals. Note that there is no access from here to the geysers.

✚ 137 A5
Te Puia
✉ Hemo Road, Rotorua ☎ 07 348 9047; www.tepuia.com ⊙ Oct–Mar daily 8–6; Apr–Sep daily 8–5 ✋ Moderate; guided tours included in admission hourly summer 9–5; winter 9–4 🍴 *Hangi* (part of evening cultural tour) 🚌 Minibus transfers from Rotorua visitor centre
Whakarewarewa Thermal Village
✉ Tryon Street, Rotorua ☎ 07 349 3463; www.whakarewarewa.com ⊙ Daily 8:30–5 ✋ Moderate; includes cultural performances at 11:15, 2 🍴 *Hangi* daily 12–2:30

5 Abel Tasman National Park

Near the top of the South Island, this is neither New Zealand's largest nor grandest national park, but it remains one of the most popular.

The park is named after the first known European to see New Zealand, and its coastal location offers a stunning combination of native bush and golden-sand beaches. Access is via Kaiteriteri and Marahau to the south, and Wainui and Totaranui to the north. Road access within the park is limited – explore instead on foot or by sea kayak.

The easy and popular coastal path is one of the most beautiful in the country and takes three to four days to walk. Be sure to plan and watch out for tides if cutting across the lagoons. There are Department of Conservation huts and camp sites for overnight stays; passes should be purchased beforehand. Launches and water taxis also serve the bays so walkers can tackle short sections.

Inland, the higher areas are more rugged. Harwood's Hole at Canaan is a sinkhole and is the deepest vertical shaft in New Zealand.

There are two other national parks in the region. Kahurangi (► 104) in the northwest can be traversed via the Heaphy Track, a good four-day hike, while Nelson Lakes National Park (► 106) to the south is known for the twin lakes of Rotoiti and Rotoroa. Surrounded by mountains and forests, the park offers boating, fishing, bush walks, and, in the winter, skiing at the Rainbow and Mount Robert ski fields. For the more experienced, there are demanding alpine climbs.

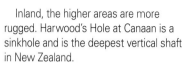

🚩 139 A6 ✉ Northwest of Nelson, via SH60 ☎ Abel Tasman Track hut reservations: 03 528 0005; www.doc.govt.nz 🕐 All year 🎫 Free access; fee for huts and camp sites 🍴 Awaroa Lodge ($$$); no road access; www.awaroalodge.co.nz 🚌 Daily tour buses from Nelson and Picton to Marahau, Kaiteriteri and Totaranui 🚢 Boat services from Nelson, Kaiteriteri and Marahau ❓ Reduced transport facilities in winter
🛈 Wallace Street, Motueka ☎ 03 528 6543

Cape Reinga

A lighthouse at Cape Reinga, New Zealand's northernmost accessible point, guards the merging waters of the Tasman Sea and the Pacific Ocean.

From the promontory there are views of the coast, which sweeps away in a combination of cliffs and sand dunes. This is the departure point for Maori spirits returning to their legendary home of 'Hawaiki'.

Part of the thrill of a visit to Cape Reinga is the journey there. It's 121km (75 miles) north of Kaitaia and 225km (140 miles) beyond Paihia, from where most buses depart. You can drive, but one-day bus tours are popular as they include stops at a kauri forest and some include a 60km (37-mile) stretch along the misnamed Ninety Mile Beach on the western side of the peninsula. Rental vehicles are forbidden on this beach. Access at the northern end is via a stream-bed with quicksand, and buses are the only vehicles allowed to cross. Nearby are giant sand dunes, which more adventurous visitors can surf down on boogie boards. There are few facilities here to detract from the spectacular setting. More amenities are 23km (14 miles) south at Waitiki Landing.

🕂 134 A1 ✉ Northern tip of the North Island, via SH1
🖐 Free access 🍴 At Waitiki Landing ($$) 🚌 Daily tours
from Kaitaia, Paihia and Mangonui
ℹ️ Jaycee Park, South Road, Kaitaia ☎ 09 408 0879;
www.fndc.govt.nz/infocentre

7

Queenstown's Skyline Gondola

www.skyline.co.nz

One of the highlights of the South Island's premier tourist area is a ride high above the town on the Skyline Gondola.

The many attractions of Queenstown and its surrounding area are featured later in the book (➤ 110), but one of the most enjoyable things to do is to take a ride on the Skyline Gondola cableway, which opened in 1967. The commanding view from the hilltop makes this a good way to get your bearings.

The ride itself, lasting just four minutes, takes visitors 450m (1,500ft) up the steep flank of Bob's Peak in small gondolas suspended from overhead cables. From the viewing platform at the top, the breathtaking scenes encompass Queenstown, Lake Wakatipu and the mountains of the Remarkables range.

The complex at the upper terminal houses a restaurant,

café and bar, and in the evenings Kiwi Haka, a cultural show, is staged. You can also do a bungy jump here, or take a chairlift ride above the complex and shoot back down along an 800m (875yd) track in a three-wheeled luge.

✚ 140 C3 ✉ Brecon Street, Queenstown ☎ 03 441 0101
🕐 Gondola: daily 9–late; Kiwi Haka: daily 5:15, 6, 7:15, 8;
luge: daily 9:30–30 minutes before dusk ✋ Gondola:
moderate; Kiwi Haka: moderate; luge: inexpensive; bungy:
expensive 🍴 Café ($), restaurant ($$) and bar

8 The TranzAlpine

www.tranzalpine.co.nz

Crossing the Southern Alps via mountain passes, tunnels and viaducts, this single-track line links the east and west coasts of the South Island.

A success story of the privately operated rail system in New Zealand has been the promotion of the scenic route from Christchurch, through the Southern Alps, to the West Coast town of Greymouth. The TranzAlpine has become a popular tourist service, as a one-way link between the coasts, and as a round-trip excursion from Christchurch. The narrow-gauge train is diesel-hauled and the carriages have large picture windows; there is also a carriage with open sides for viewing and photography.

Departing daily from Christchurch in the morning, the train crosses the farmlands of the Canterbury Plains, passing through a number of small towns before stopping at Springfield. From here the journey is spectacular, as the train continues over viaducts and through tunnels across the Canterbury foothills up to Arthur's Pass. At 737m (2,417ft), this is the highest railroad station in the South Island and sees the arrival of many visitors bound for Arthur's Pass National Park, which offers numerous opportunities for hiking and mountaineering.

Shortly after leaving here, the train enters the 8km (5-mile) Otira Tunnel for the descent to Otira. On this side of the Southern Alps, the rainforests and scrubby landscapes of Westland offer a contrast to the eastern side. The line continues past mountains and along valleys before running beside the Grey River into Greymouth. The train returns to Christchurch in the afternoon.

✚ 139 E5 ✉ Christchurch station, Troup Drive, Addington
☎ 04 495 0775 ⏱ Departs Christchurch daily 8:15am, return arrival 6:05pm 🖐 Expensive 🍴 Refreshments available on train ($) 🚆 Christchurch; Greymouth

9 Aoraki/Mount Cook National Park

www.mtcooknz.com

New Zealand's highest peak, Aoraki/Mount Cook, forms the centrepiece of this beautiful alpine area in the heart of the South Island.

Much of the South Island is mountainous and the Southern Alps mountain range forms a backbone for most of the island's length. Of some 220 named peaks above 2,300m (7,500ft) in New Zealand, the highest, at 3,754m (12,313ft), commemorates both a Maori god and the English navigator who first landed in

New Zealand in 1769. Nearby Mount Tasman is the second-highest peak, at 3,498m (11,473ft).

Aoraki/Mount Cook lies in the Aoraki/Mount Cook National Park, adjacent to Westland National Park. These two parks, together with Mount Aspiring (➤ 128) and Fiordland (➤ 26–27) national parks, have been incorporated into a UNESCO World Heritage Area.

Most of the alpine terrain of Aoraki/Mount Cook National Park is popular with trekkers and climbers. These mountains – 19 of them exceeding 3,000m (9,800ft) – offer a spectacular panorama of peaks, glaciers and rivers from trails of varying difficulty. Flights in

ski-equipped light aircraft are popular, taking in views of Aoraki/Mount Cook and the Alps, and include a landing on the snowfield of the Tasman Glacier – one of the longest glaciers in the world's temperate zones at 27km (17 miles).

Most coach tours include Mount Cook Village (dominated by the Hermitage Hotel), either looping in as a day trip, or staying a night or two.

✚ 138 F4 ✉ At the end of SH80, 333km (206 miles) west of Christchurch 🖐 Free access 🍴 Hermitage Hotel, Mount Cook Village ($$–$$$) 🚌 Buses from Christchurch and Queenstown
🛈 1 Larch Grove, Aoraki/Mount Cook
☎ 03 435 1186 🕔 Nov–Mar daily 8:30–5

10 Waitomo Caves

www.waitomoinfo.co.nz

These are among New Zealand's most impressive natural wonders. Glow-worms twinkle like stars on the roof of a cave above an underground river.

The caves are some 200km (120 miles) south of Auckland, at the end of SH37 between the towns of Otorohanga and Te Kuiti. In the area are a number of rocky outcrops, with a labyrinth of caves and channels beneath. The two main caves open to the public are the Waitomo Glowworm Caves and the Aranui Cave. The former, which have given their name to the area, are the more popular. Visitors in guided parties are led through subterranean chambers of varying sizes containing delicate limestone stalactite and stalagmite formations highlighted by special lighting effects.

The main attraction of the Waitomo Glowworm Caves, however, is the boat ride along an underground stream into a cave where you can gaze up at thousands of glow-worms lighting up the roof like stars. The effect is created by the 'lights' that the tiny insect larvae create to lure prey into their mesh of sticky mucus threads.

The Aranui Cave is worth visiting for its beautiful limestone formations, although it does not have the bonus of glow-worms. The quieter Ruakuri Cave has glow-worms as well as an underground river; this is the scene of many black-water rafting tours.

The caves are usually busy with coach tours in the middle of the day, so try to avoid this time. At the visitor centre, the Museum of Caves has good

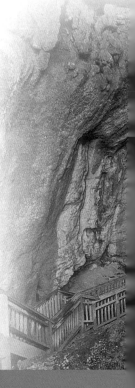

audiovisual displays. Except for a hotel, there are few facilities near the caves.

✚ 136 A4 ✉ On SH37, 8km (5 miles) off SH3, south of Otorohanga ☎ 07 878 7640 🕐 Oct–Easter Mon daily 9–5:30; rest of year daily 9–5 ✋ Expensive 🍴 Waitomo Caves Hotel ($$) 🚐 Minibus transfers from intercity buses 🚉 Transfers from Otorohanga station ❓ Included in most North Island coach tours

Exploring

New Zealand is in the South Pacific, 2,000km (1,200 miles) from Australia and at the opposite end of the world as far as many visitors are concerned. Today the country's remoteness, pristine environment and lack of crowds have made it particularly attractive to tourists. Combine this with modern communications and transport networks, and it's easy to see why tourist numbers have shot up.

Visitors who arrive on New Zealand's shores will not be disappointed, for this is a country that packs a lot into its relatively small area. North Island, the smaller of the two main islands, has historic sights to visit, volcanoes and geysers, and a vibrant Maori cultural scene. It is also home to Auckland and Wellington, the two largest cities. The South Island, meanwhile, is renowned for its dramatic mountain scenery, wilderness areas and unique flora and fauna.

Upper North Island

Auckland

This quarter of New Zealand, which includes the largest city, Auckland, is home to more than half the country's population. In 1840, New Zealand's founding document, the Treaty of Waitangi, was signed by Maori chiefs and representatives of the British Crown in the Bay of Islands. Near the northern tip of Northland is Cape Reinga, where Maori spirits of the deceased are said to depart for their ancient Polynesian home.

One hour east of Auckland is the Coromandel Peninsula, a beautiful but rugged area of forest trails, old gold mines, deserted beaches and arts and crafts outlets. There's plenty on offer to suit everyone and a range of activities and sights.

About three hours' drive southeast of Auckland is Rotorua, the heart of traditional Maori culture in a geothermally active region of lakes, forests and volcanic remnants.

Farther south, in the middle of the North Island, is the resort town of Taupo, which can be found nestling on the shore of Lake Taupo with a distant view of the brooding volcanoes of magnificent Tongariro National Park.

AUCKLAND

The city, built over the dormant remnants of 48 volcanoes, sprawls across a narrow isthmus between the Pacific Ocean and the Tasman Sea, beach and bush readily at hand. With a population of 1.3 million, it is New Zealand's largest and most cosmopolitan city as well as being the main commercial and industrial base. Auckland also offers an array of cultural and sporting activities.

Auckland is the major New Zealand gateway for air and sea passengers, and there are road, rail and long-distance bus services to most parts of the North Island.

European settlement began here in 1840, and it was New Zealand's capital until 1865. The compact downtown area is still its hub, but there are major shopping and entertainment areas beyond the central streets, and the attractions for visitors spread to and beyond the suburbs.

www.aucklandnz.com

🗺 134 D4

ℹ SkyCity, corner of Victoria and Federal streets ☎ 09 367 6009

Albert Park

Conveniently situated close to downtown Auckland, this formal garden has a Victorian pavilion and statuary among its many flowerbeds and trees, just waiting to be discovered.

Unsurprisingly it is well used as a shady retreat by city office workers and students from the Auckland University campus looking for a little rest and relaxation.

➕ 143 C5 ✉ Princes Street ☎ 09 307 7604 🕐 Unrestricted
🖐 Free access

Aotea Centre

Found on central Aotea Square, this building houses a concert hall, a conference centre, exhibition areas, restaurants and bars. There is also a reservations office for major Auckland events and concerts: check what's on during your stay.

The Auckland Town Hall, built in 1911, now serves as another concert venue. Also adjacent is the Entertainment Centre with its giant IMAX cinema screen.

➕ 142 C4 ✉ Aotea Square, Queen Street ☎ 09 309 2677; www.the-edge.co.nz 🕐 Daily 8:30–6 🍴 Limelight ($$)

Auckland Art Gallery

Located within a Victorian edifice, the main gallery displays a prominent collection of New Zealand and overseas paintings, prints and drawings. Important touring exhibitions from overseas are also shown here (admission charge). Opposite is the New Gallery (inexpensive), an annex of contemporary art, and nearby is the Auckland Central Public Library, which houses a collection of historic and rare books.

www.aucklandartgallery.govt.nz

➕ 143 C5 ✉ Corner of Wellesley and Kitchener streets ☎ 09 307 7700 🕓 Daily 10–5 🖐 Free 🍴 Art Gallery Café ($$); Reuben ($$) ❓ Free guided tour 2pm

Auckland Zoo

Near the Museum of Transport and Technology (➤ 56), and connected to it by vintage tram, Auckland's zoo houses the usual overseas creatures plus native species such as the kiwi and indigenous birds in a forest aviary. There's a farm animal section for children and Pridelands, a simulated African savannah enclosure with giraffes, zebras and other animals. The zoo's endangered species programme is internationally recognized.

www.aucklandzoo.co.nz

➕ 142 F1 (off map) ✉ Motions Road, Western Springs
☎ 09 360 3800 🕓 Oct–Apr daily 9:30–5:30; May–Sep daily 9:30–5; last admission 4:15 🖐 Moderate 🍴 Café and kiosks ($) 🚌 045

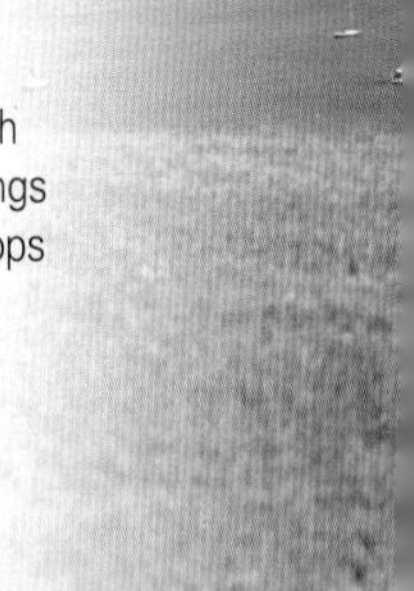

Devonport

Ten minutes across the harbour, in the attractive North Shore suburb of Devonport many 19th-century buildings house cafés, book shops, craft galleries, antiques shops and a couple of museums.

➕ 143 A7 (off map) ⛴ Ferries from Quay Street: Fullers
☎ 09 367 9111; www.fullers.co.nz
ℹ 3 Victoria Road, Devonport ☎ 09 446 0677

The Domain and Auckland Museum

The Domain's 75ha (185 acres) of parkland lie between downtown and Newmarket. The Wintergardens display exotic plants in a hot-house and there is also a dell of New Zealand ferns. In the Domain, the impressive Auckland Museum houses extensive collections of Maori and Polynesian objects, the flora and fauna of New Zealand, arts and crafts from other countries, and a war memorial display. The museum often hosts special exhibitions.

✚ Domain: 143 D6; Museum: 143 E6 ✉ Museum: Auckland Domain, Parnell
☎ 09 306 7067; www.aucklandmuseum.com ◷ Daily 10–5 🍴 Two cafés ($)
✋ Free; charge for exhibitions and concerts ❓ Maori concerts 11, 12, 1:30 daily, plus 2:30 in summer

Harbour Bridge

Arching across Waitemata Harbour (➤ 59) to the North Shore
suburbs, the bridge is more than 1km (0.5 miles) long. It opened
in 1959 with four lanes, later widened to eight. Harbour cruises
go under it and sightseeing buses go over it, but there's no access
for pedestrians – except for bridge-climbers and bungy-jumpers.
🛟 142 A1 (off map) ☎ 09 361 2000 (Auckland Bridge Climb);
www.ajhackett.com ⏰ Trips daily at 9, 11:30, 2:30. Closed public holidays
except Easter 💷 Expensive ❓ Views of the bridge from Shelly Beach Road
and Westhaven Drive; beware of one-way streets

Kelly Tarlton's Antarctic Encounter and Underwater World

This aquarium has walk-through transparent acrylic tunnels and more than 2,000 fish and other marine animals, including sharks from the waters around New Zealand. Next door is Stingray Bay, home to Phoebe, a 2m (6.5ft) stingray.

There is also a ride through a re-creation of an Antarctic landscape, with a replica of explorer Captain Scott's 1911 hut and a colony of penguins.

www.kellytarltons.co.nz

🔂 143 C8 ✉ 23 Tamaki Drive, Orakei ☎ 09 528 0603 🕐 Daily 9–6 (last admission 5) 👐 Moderate 🍴 Refreshment Kiosk ($) 🚌 Free shuttle daily on the hour 9–4 from Sky City Hotel forecourt

Mount Eden and One Tree Hill

Respectively the highest (196m/643ft) and second highest (183m/600ft) of Auckland's mainland volcanic peaks, both provide panoramic views. Roads go to the top of both, but most sightseeing tours opt for Mount Eden. Both were former Maori *pa* (fortresses), and terracing and storage pits are still visible.

🚹 142 F4 (off map) ✉ Mount Eden: access off Hillside Crescent, Mount Eden Road; One Tree Hill: access off Manukau Road at Royal Oak
🕐 Unrestricted access

Museum of Transport and Technology

This museum, spread over two sites, displays vintage cars, aircraft, trams, colonial buildings and other technological items

from yesteryear, largely maintained by volunteer groups. Exhibits include a replica of Richard Pearse's aircraft, which reputedly flew near Timaru earlier than the Wright brothers' more famous flight; and the only Solent Mark IV flying boat left in the world. Admission includes a return ride to Auckland Zoo (➤ 52) on a historic tram.

www.motat.org.nz

✚ 142 F1 (off map) ✉ 805 Great North Road, Western Springs
☎ 09 815 5800 ◷ Daily 10–5 🖐 Moderate 🍴 Café ($) 🚌 045

New Zealand National Maritime Museum

New Zealand has a considerable maritime heritage, and this is displayed inside old warehouses next to the waterfront. Exhibits range from Polynesian canoes to America's Cup yachts, and

there are workshops where crafts are demonstrated. Take a trip on an old steam launch, and visit the marina.

www.nzmaritime.org

✚ 142 B4 ✉ Corner of Quay and Hobson Streets ☎ 09 373 0800
◷ Oct–Apr daily 9–6; Mar–Sep daily 9–5 🖐 Moderate

Sky Tower

The tallest structure in the southern hemisphere at 328m (1,076ft) the tower has three observation decks, two restaurants and bar, and a glass floorplate. Those with a head for heights can try the 192m (630ft) Sky Jump, which involves a 16-second freefall.

www.skycity.co.nz

✚ 142 C4 ✉ Corner of Victoria and Federal streets ☎ 09 363 6000;
◷ Sun–Thu 8:30am–11pm, Fri–Sat 8:30am–midnight 🖐 Moderate
🍴 Observatory and Orbit ($$$) restaurants

Around Auckland

AUCKLAND BOTANIC GARDENS

These 64ha (158-acre) gardens south of the city house some 10,000 exotic and native plants. If your time is limited, visit Eden Garden, on the eastern flank of Mount Eden (➤ 56).

www.aucklandbotanicgardens.co.nz

✚ 134 E4 ✉ 102 Hill Road, Manurewa; south of Auckland ☎ 09 267 1457 🕐 Daily 8–8 (mid–Mar–mid Oct daily 8–6) ✋ Free 🍴 Café ($$)

WAITAKERE RANGES

A picturesque route, with bush scenery and views across the city, winds through the forested hills to Auckland's west. Signposted as Scenic Route 24, the drive starts at New Lynn and passes

through Titirangi to **Arataki Visitor Centre,** where cantilevered platforms provide breathtaking views of the rainforest and Manukau Harbour. Inside the centre are informative displays about the wildlife and plants of the area. You can also drive on to the beautiful ocean beaches of Piha, Karekare, Bethells (Te Henga) and Muriwai, where you can see a gannet colony close up.

✚ 134 E3

Arataki Visitor Centre

☎ 09 817 0077 🕔 Oct–Apr daily 9–5; May–Sep Mon–Fri 10–4, Sat–Sun 9–5 ✋ Free

WAITEMATA HARBOUR AND HAURAKI GULF

Waitemata Harbour, on the northern side of the isthmus, opens onto the Hauraki Gulf. You can get there by fast and frequent catamarans, ferries, launches and yachts from the Ferry Terminal on Quay Street.

The most popular of the Hauraki Gulf islands is Waiheke, 35 minutes from Auckland by fast ferry. Craft shops, vineyards and superb beaches are among its numerous attractions.

The volcanic cone of Rangitoto is the nearest island to the city. The last eruption that occurred here is the most recent in the region and is thought to have taken place sometime within the past 600 years. You can take a safari tour to just below the summit, or you can walk to the crater in about one hour.

✚ 143 A6 🚢 Regular ferries and boat tours: Fullers ☎ 09 367 9111; www.fullers.co.nz ✋ Cruise prices vary 🍴 Cin Cin on Quay ($$$) and Harbourside Seafood Bar and Grill ($$$)

a drive through suburban Auckland

Starting from the Ferry Terminal on Quay Street, this drive heads east around the bays of Tamaki Drive to St Heliers, then loops inland to the suburbs of Remuera and Newmarket before returning via Parnell to Quay Street.

Tamaki Drive passes the public Parnell Swimming Baths and Okahu Bay. Kelly Tarlton's Antarctic Encounter and Underwater World (➤ 55) is a worthwhile stop.

Continue to Mission Bay, a popular swimming beach and an area of busy cafés. A short walk to the Bastion Point headland provides vistas of the harbour and Hauraki Gulf (➤ 59). Drive on to Kohimarama and the waterfront village of St Heliers.

Turn right onto St Heliers Bay Road. Follow this up the hill to the St Johns Road traffic lights, where you turn left onto St Johns Road, then right at the traffic circle.

This leads to Remuera Road and through the wealthy suburb of Remuera, to the fashionable entertainment and shopping area of Newmarket. Turn right on Broadway and continue straight on to Parnell Road. Domain Drive on your left leads to the Domain and Auckland Museum ➤ 53).

You could take a one-hour stroll down Parnell Road, parking if possible near the Anglican Cathedral at the top of the road. The area around the colonial-style Parnell Village has many restaurants, cafés, craft shops and boutiques.

Continue driving, turning right just past the cathedral into St Stephens Avenue and turn left onto Gladstone Road. Pause for a breather at the Rose Gardens and a view of the harbour before returning to the Ferry Building.

Distance 24km (15 miles)
Time 1 hour plus stops; suggest at least half a day
Start/end point Ferry Terminal, Quay Street ✚ 143 B5
Lunch Lava Restaurant & Bar ($$) ✉ 425 Tamaki Drive, St Heliers
☎ 09 575 9969

More to see in the Upper North Island

BAY OF ISLANDS

In addition to being one of New Zealand's most historically interesting regions for both Europeans and Maori, this is among the North Island's most popular resort areas. The Bay of Islands Maritime and Historic Park consists of more than 800km (500 miles) of coastline and some 150 islands, as well as many reserves on the surrounding mainland and the communities of Paihia, Russell and Kerikeri.

✚ 134 B3   ℹ The Wharf, Marsden Road, Paihia
☎ 09 402 7345

Kerikeri

Kerikeri, 23km (14 miles) from Paihia, is known for its citrus orchards and craft workshops. It is the small harbour basin, however, that is of most interest. Historic sites here include the **Mission House,** erected in 1822 as the country's second mission station and now the oldest surviving building in New Zealand; and the **Stone Store,** originally part of the mission settlement but now a museum. Across the inlet is **Rewa's Village,** a reconstruction of a pre-European Maori fishing village.

➕ 134 B3

Mission House and Stone Store
✉ Kerikeri Basin ☎ 09 407 9236
🕐 Nov–Apr daily 10–5; May–Oct
daily 10–4 💲 Inexpensive

Rewa's Village
✉ Landing Road ☎ 09 407 6454
🕐 Nov–Mar daily 9–5; May–Oct daily
10–4 💲 Inexpensive

Paihia

Paihia sprawls over three bays.
Its town centre is the wharf, from
where various scenic and nature
cruises depart, as well as a
regular passenger service across
to Russell (➤ 64). Restaurants,
accommodation and cafés
are plentiful.

From the southern end of
Paihia, the Opua-Paihia Coastal
Walkway is an attractive 5.8km
(3.5-mile) walk – allow about 2–3
hours each way. The scenery
includes sandy beaches and
mangrove boardwalks. Adjacent
to the walkway is Harrison's Bush
Scenic Reserve, one of the area's
best examples of coastal forest.
www.northlandnz.com

➕ 134 B3

ℹ The Wharf, Marsden Road
☎ 09 402 7345

Russell

Russell, New Zealand's first European settlement, was
known as 'the hell-hole of the Pacific' back in the days
when lawless whalers came into violent contact with
local Maori and each other. The town is now a quiet
hamlet, although the bullet holes in the 1836 wooden
church and the graves in its churchyard testify to its
lively past. Other sights include the 1842 **Pompallier,**
built as part of the French Catholic mission, and nearby
Flagstaff Hill – scene of disputes between British troops
and local Maori in the 1840s. The **Russell Museum** has
a one-fifth scale model of Cook's ship *Endeavour*.

✚ 134 B3

Pompallier

✉ The Strand ☎ 09 403 7861 🕓 Dec–Apr daily 10–5;
May–Nov guided tours daily 👤 Inexpensive

Russell Museum

✉ 2 York Street ☎ 09 403 7701 🕓 Feb–Dec daily 10–4; Jan
daily 10–5 👤 Inexpensive

Waitangi Historic Reserve

Just north of Paihia is the Waitangi Historic Reserve, where, in
1840, a treaty was signed by Maori chiefs and the British Crown
under the auspices of Captain (later Governor) William Hobson. The
treaty promised the Maori people rights in exchange for British
sovereignty, but its interpretation remains controversial today. The
Treaty House, built in 1834 for the British government official, is
open to visitors. The Waitangi Treaty Grounds also display a
centennial (1940) Maori meeting house and a 36m (169ft) Maori
waka (war canoe), and there are cultural performances and tours.

www.waitangi.net.nz

✚ 134 B3 ✉ Tau Henare Drive, near Paihia ☎ 09 402 7437
🕓 Oct–May daily 9–6; Jun–Sep daily 9–5 👤 Moderate
🍴 Waikokopu Café ($$)

COROMANDEL PENINSULA

A good place to start your Coromandel trip is Thames, a town with a gold-mining past that now acts as a gateway to the peninsula. From here SH25 meanders north up the west coast, over forested volcanic hills, to the town of Coromandel. This centre for arts and crafts also has a boating and fishing harbour.

Over on the east coast, don't miss stunning Cathedral Cove, which is great for snorkelling and diving, and Hot Water Beach, where you can dig your own private spa in the sand. Captain Cook anchored the *Endeavour* off nearby Cooks Beach in 1769 to observe the transit of the planet Mercury across the sun.

www.thecoromandel.com

⊞ 135 D5

ℹ 206 Pollen Street, Thames ☎ 07 868 7284

NORTHLAND

In the subtropical far north of New Zealand you will find the country's longest beach, as well as its tallest trees – the impressive kauri at Waipoua Forest Park.

✚ 134 B3

Cape Reinga

Best places to see, ▶ 36–37.

Waipoua Kauri Forest

This forest is a remnant of the bush that once covered nearly all the Northland region. New Zealand kauri is one of the world's oldest-growing and largest trees, with a long straight trunk; its golden timber was highly prized, and its gum used to make lacquer. The scenic road through the reserve passes many of these trees, but the largest, called Tane Mahuta, is reached via a short bush walk.

✚ 134 B2 ✉ SH12; 112km (69 miles) from Paihia ③ Unrestricted ✋ Free
ℹ Waipoua ☎ 09 439 3011; www.doc.govt.nz

ROTORUA

The city of Rotorua, 234km (145 miles) southeast of Auckland, is recognized as the North Island's leading tourist centre because of its Maori culture, scenic variety and geothermal activity. The latter becomes apparent in the form of sulphurous odours near the city. Whakarewarewa (▶ 32) is the city's leading geothermal reserve, but the area has a number of other places with such activity, plus a dozen lakes, an evergreen forest and a host of other attractions (▶ 67–71). The main shopping thoroughfare is Tutanekai Street.

www.rotoruanz.com
✚ 137 A5
🛈 1167 Fenton Street ☎ 07 348 5179

Agrodome

Here the story of sheep in the New Zealand economy is told with regular sheep-shearing displays, lamb feeding, mock sheep auctions, and sheep and cattle shows. Tours of the farm are available and you can buy woollen goods at the shop.

www.agrodome.co.nz

✚ 137 A5 ✉ Western Road, Ngongotaha ☎ 07 357 1050 ⏰ Daily 8:30–5; shows 9.30, 11, 2:30 ✋ Moderate

Hell's Gate and the Waiyora Spa

The reserve here covers about 20ha (50 acres), and an extensive walk takes visitors past pools of hot water, bubbling mud and other features. Irish playwright George Bernard Shaw is supposed to have given the area its name on seeing it. The spa offers several thermal water and mud baths and treatments.

www.hellsgate.co.nz

🕂 137 A6 ✉ SH30, Tikitere; 18km (11 miles) northeast of Rotorua ☎ 07 345 3151 🕒 Daily 8:30–8:30 👋 Moderate

Lake Rotorua

This is the largest of a dozen or so lakes in the region, and can be explored on a cruise or self-drive rental boat. Mokoia Island, in the middle of the lake, is the setting for a Maori legend about two young lovers who were called Hinemoa and Tutanekai.

www.rotoruanz.com

🕂 137 A5 ℹ 1167 Fenton Street, Rotorua ☎ 07 348 5179

Ohinemutu

Ohinemutu, a Maori village on the shore of Lake Rotorua, was once the main settlement here. It is of interest for its Anglican **St Faith's Church** (notice the window showing Christ dressed in a Maori cloak), and a carved Maori meeting house (not open to the public).

St Faith's Church

✉ Mataiawhea Street 🕒 Daily 9–4:30

👋 Free, or donation

ℹ 1167 Fenton Street, Rotorua ☎ 07 348 5179

Rainbow Springs Nature Park

The natural freshwater springs welling up here on the side of Mount Ngongotaha are stocked with four species of trout that can be observed in the fern-fringed pools and fed with fish food. Also at the park are tuatara and several native birds, including kiwis in a specially designed enclosure. Night-time tours see the kiwis emerge into the open.

www.rainbowsprings.co.nz
✉ Fairy Springs Road
☎ 07 350 0440 🕐 Oct–May daily 8am–11pm; Jun–Sep 8am–10pm. Kiwi Encounter tours: daily 10–4 ✋ Moderate
🍴 Café ($)

Skyline Skyrides

Mount Ngongotaha (757m/2,483ft) is a prominent peak on the western shore of Lake Rotorua. Although there is a road to the top, the Skyrides gondola is a popular attraction, taking passengers 180m (590ft) to a viewpoint halfway up the mountain, offering a panorama of the city and lake. At the top you can race part of the way back down on a three-wheel luge along one of three tracks, returning to the top on a chairlift.

www.skylineskyrides.co.nz
✉ Fairy Springs Road
☎ 07 347 0027 🕐 Daily 9–late
✋ Moderate 🍴 Café ($); restaurant ($$)

Te Wairoa Buried Village

In 1886 the dormant volcano of Mount Tarawera erupted, resulting in loss of life and the destruction of three villages – Te Wairoa, Moura, and Te Ariki – which were buried under ash and mud.

Also obliterated were the famous Pink and White Terraces, fan-like natural silica formations on the shores of Lake Rotomahana. The village of Te Wairoa has since been partly excavated, and may be seen separately or as part of a round-trip visit incorporating other sites.

Tours of the volcano can be arranged at Rotorua's visitor centre in Fenton Street.

www.buriedvillage.co.nz

✚ 137 A5 ✉ Tarawera Road; 14km (8.5 miles) from Rotorua
☎ 07 362 8287 ⏰ Nov–Mar daily 8:30–5:30; Apr–Oct daily 9–4:30 🚌 Free shuttle from Rotorua Visitor Centre daily 9:30
✋ Moderate

Waimangu Volcanic Valley

Waimangu also has impressive volcanic activity. There is a walk past thermal pools, including Frying Pan Lake, the world's largest hot-water spring, and a path leads down to Lake Rotomahana, where cruises sail past steaming cliffs and over the sunken site of the Pink and White Terraces (➤ above). A round-trip tour links this lake with Lake Tarawera, returning to Rotorua via Te Wairoa Buried Village (➤ above).

www.waimangu.com

➕ 137 A5 ✉ Off SH5; 19km (11.5 miles) south of Rotorua ☎ 07 366 6137 🕐 Feb–Dec daily 8:30–5 (last admission 3:45); Jan daily 8:30–6 (last admission 4:45) ✋ Moderate

Wai-O-Tapu Thermal Wonderland

The most colourful of the geothermal areas, Wai-O-Tapu encompasses thermal zones that have been given their different hues by mineral deposits. Highlights include the Lady Knox Geyser, which erupts every morning at 10:15 and can reach heights of 20m (65.5ft), and the hot Champagne Pool.

There are three different walks around the main park. Graphic displays provide basic information on volcanic activity, fauna and flora.

www.geyserland.co.nz

➕ 137 A5 ✉ Off SH5; 27km (16.5 miles) south of Rotorua ☎ 07 366 6333 🕐 Daily 8:30–5 (last admission 3:45) ✋ Moderate

Whakarewarewa Thermal Reserve

Best places to see, ➤ 32–33.

TAUPO

The town of Taupo nestles at the heart of the North Island beside Lake Taupo, looking out towards the distant peaks of the Tongariro National Park. Together with the surrounding area, it has become a major holiday destination and offers visitors a wealth of attractions.

www.laketauponz.com

✚ 137 B5 🚹 Tongariro Street ☎ 07 376 0027

Huka Falls

Near Wairakei, where the Waikato River plunges over an 11m (36ft) drop, are the Huka Falls. The huge volume of water that crashes through this narrow defile makes it a thunderous spectacle. There are various vantage points along the path.

✚ 137 B5 ✉ Off SH1; 3km (2 miles) north of Taupo 🔘 Unrestricted access

🖐 Free 🚹 Tongariro Street, Taupo ☎ 07 376 0027

Lake Taupo

Formed predominantly by two massive volcanic eruptions, 26,500 years ago and in AD181, Lake Taupo, covering 600sq km (232sq miles), is the largest lake in New Zealand.

The lake is internationally renowned for its trout fishing, and fishing guides and charter boats are available. There are also cruises on the lake and along parts of the Waikato River, New Zealand's longest waterway, which flows north out of Lake Taupo.

✚ 137 B5 🚢 Lake cruises depart from Taupo Marina
ℹ Tongariro Street, Taupo ☎ 07 376 0027

Waipahihi Botanical Gardens

This 34ha (85-acre) drive-through reserve has walks lined with native trees, and beds of stunning rhododendrons and azaleas. The gardens are at their very best when the shrubs are in full flower during October.

✚ 137 B5 ✉ Shepherd Road ☎ 07 378 9417 🕐 Daily during daylight hours
✋ Free

Wairakei Terraces

The geothermal energy of the Wairakei Valley was first harnessed back in 1958, and visitors today can tour the geothermal field from the Wairakei Terraces visitor centre. The terraces themselves are a man-made re-creation of the natural silica formations that existed here before the development of the power station. Also on site are evening cultural tours, based around a re-created Maori village.

✚ 137 B5 ✉ Intersection of SH1 and SH5, 10km (6 miles) north of Taupo
☎ 03 378 0913 🕐 Oct–Mar daily 9–5; Apr–Sep daily 9–4:30 ✋ Expensive
🍴 Café ($); *hangi* as part of evening tour

WAITOMO CAVES

Best places to see, ► 44–45.

Lower North Island

**South of Lake Taupo the North
Island becomes considerably
hillier. Tongariro National Park, the
oldest national park in New Zealand, is
dominated by a trio of volcanoes,
marking the southern edge of the
volcanic belt.**

Wellington

In the west, the city of New Plymouth is watched over by its
dormant volcano, Mount Taranaki. In the east, the hills of Hawke's
Bay, a horticultural, wine-growing and sheep-farming region,
sweep down to the twin cities of Napier and Hastings. In
between, the navigable Whanganui River is steeped in Maori
history, and you can canoe most of its 329km (204-mile) length
and see the country from a different angle. Down at the southern
tip of the island lies the vibrant capital city of Wellington, guarding
Cook Strait.

   Within easy reach of the capital is the Wairarapa, where the
small town of Martinborough has several boutique wineries.
Beyond, a road leads to Palliser Bay and Cape Palliser, where there
are rugged, remote beaches.

WELLINGTON

European settlement started here in 1840 and, since its selection as New Zealand's capital in 1865, Wellington hasn't looked back.

At the southern tip of the North Island, Wellington is a commercial hub with excellent transport links. It's also the nation's cultural centre, home to the New Zealand Symphony Orchestra, the Royal New Zealand Ballet Company and Te Papa Tongarewa, the Museum of New Zealand and a thriving entertainment scene. Bounded on three sides by the sea and inland by circling hills, Wellington is a compact city, easy to get around on foot, and its deep harbour acts as a focal point. There are plenty of parks, gardens and hilly viewpoints, in addition to the beaches.

Within Wellington there is the distinctive heart, including its parliament and government offices; the Hutt Valley – largely residential, but with industry at its southern end; and the northern satellite city of Porirua and the beaches of the Kapiti Coast.

www.wellingtonnz.com

✚ 136 F3

ℹ Civic Square, corner of Victoria and Wakefield streets ☎ 04 802 4860

Botanic Garden

Spread over 25ha (62 acres), this garden includes both native bush and exotic plants. The Lady Norwood Rose Garden, with more than 100 different species of rose, and the Begonia House are additional features. At the top of the hill (near the Cable Car terminal) is the Carter Observatory, with a planetarium, astonomical displays, telescopes and a hands-on area.

www.wbg.co.nz

✚ 144 C1 ✉ Tinakori Road, Glenmore Street and Upland Road ☎ 04 499 1400 🕐 Daily dawn–dusk ✋ Free 🚌 Cable Car No 3 Karori bus

Cable Car

Rising from the terminal off Lambton Quay, the cable cars climb a 1-in-5 gradient to Kelburn. The service began in 1902, but the original wooden cable cars have been replaced. At the top, where there are fine views, is the appealing **Cable Car Museum.**

✚ 144 D1 ✉ Cable Car Lane, 280 Lambton Quay ☎ 04 472 2199 🕐 Mon–Fri 7am–10pm, Sat–Sun and public holidays 8:30am–10pm, every 10 minutes ✋ Inexpensive

Cable Car Museum

✉ Upper Cable Car terminus, Upland Road, Kelburn ☎ 04 475 3578; www.cablecarmuseum.co.nz 🕐 Nov–Easter Mon daily 9:30–5:30; rest of year Mon–Fri 9:30–5, Sat–Sun and public holidays 10–4:30 ✋ Free

Katherine Mansfield Birthplace

New Zealand's greatest short-story writer was born in this wooden house in 1888. Now restored, the building is open for viewing and has both permament and changing exhibitions.

www.katherinemansfield.com

✚ 144 A3 (off map) ✉ 25 Tinakori Road, Thorndon ☎ 04 473 7268 🕐 Tue–Sun 10–4 ✋ Inexpensive 🚌 No 14 Wilton bus

Museum of Wellington City and Sea
Displays on the history of Wellington city and harbour. More than 80 model ships, nautical paraphernalia, old photos and lots more, all illustrating the long maritime associations of the region.
www.museumofwellington.co.nz
✚ 144 D3 ✉ Queens Wharf ☎ 04 472 8904 🕐 Daily 10–5 ✋ Free

National Library and Archives New Zealand
The National Library contains reference copies of books and periodicals. An important part of the archive is the famous Alexander Turnbull Library, which includes perhaps the world's finest collection of works by John Milton, the 17th-century English poet.

  Nearby is Archives New Zealand, storing important historical documents, paintings, photographs and films. Exhibitions include a permanent display of the original 1840 Treaty of Waitangi.
National Library
✚ 144 B3 ✉ Corner of Molesworth and Aitken streets
☎ 04 474 3000; www.natlib.govt.nz 🕐 Mon–Fri 9–5, Sat 9–1
🍴 Short Black Café ($) ✋ Free
Archives New Zealand
✚ 144 B4 ✉ 10 Mulgrave Street ☎ 04 499 5595; www.archives.govt.nz
🕐 Mon–Fri 9–5, Sat 9–1 ✋ Free

Old St Paul's Church
The old church consecrated in 1866, so called to distinguish it from the new 1964 cathedral, is used mainly for concerts. However, its fine Gothic Revival style and its history have secured it as a property of the Historic Places Trust, safeguarding its future.
✚ 144 B3 ✉ 34 Mulgrave Street ☎ 04 473 6722; www.historic.org.nz
🕐 Daily 10–5. Closed Good Fri, 25 Dec ✋ Free; donations welcome

Parliament Buildings

The most distinctive of the Parliament Buildings complex in downtown Wellington is the Beehive, designed by Sir Basil Spence. It houses ministerial offices and the Cabinet Room. Next to it is the Parliament House, home of New Zealand's one-chamber parliament, and adjacent to this is the Parliamentary Library.

www.parliament.nz

🏛 144 B3 ✉ Pathway leads in from Lambton Quay ☎ 04 471 9503 🕐 Mon–Fri 9–5, Sat and public holidays 9:30–4, Sun 11:30–4. Free one-hour tours on the hour ✋ Free ❓ Not open for unguided sightseers

Te Papa Tongarewa

Best places to see, ▶ 30–31

Around Wellington

DAYS BAY AND EASTBOURNE

Although these village suburbs, nestling on hilly slopes on the eastern shores of Wellington's harbour, are connected to the city by road and ferry, they feel a world away. The two beaches are 15 minutes' walk apart. Behind Eastbourne village, with its cafés and craft and antiques shops, the Butterfly Creek trail is a popular local walk, while Williams Park, behind Days Bay, is popular for picnics and alfresco dining.

🚹 136 F4 ⏰ Up to 15 sailings a day 🍴 Cobar Bar and Restaurant, Days Bay ($$$) 🚌 81, 83 via Petone ⛴ The Dominion Post Ferry from Queens Wharf

FELL LOCOMOTIVE MUSEUM, FEATHERSTON

The fell engine at Featherston is a special steam locomotive that was used on the railway over the Rimutaka Range, before the tunnel was built in 1955. The **Rimutaka Rail Trail** follows the route of the former line from the edge of the Wellington conurbation. At 18km (11 miles), the walk takes four to five hours to complete.

🚹 136 E4 ✉ Corner Lyon and Fitzherbert streets, Featherston
☎ 06 308 9379 ⏰ Daily 10–4 🖐 Inexpensive

Rimutaka Rail Trail

☎ 04 384 7770 (Department of Conservation Wellington office)

KAPITI COAST

Centred on the suburbs of Paekakariki and Paraparaumu to the north of Wellington, the Kapiti Coast is known for its fine white sandy beaches and good water-sports facilities. Kapiti Island, 5km (3 miles) offshore, is a bird sanctuary with restricted access. Boat trips depart from Paraparaumu.

Southward Car Museum near Paraparaumu, has one of the largest and most extensive private collections of vintage automobiles in the southern hemisphere. It's also home to a selection of various engines and motorcycles.

136 E4 🚉 Plimmerton, Paekakariki or Paraparaumu then buses 71–74
ℹ️ Coastlands Car Park ☎ 04 298 8195; www.naturecoast.co.nz

Southward Car Museum
✉ Otaihanga Road, Paraparaumu; 55km (33 miles) north of Wellington
☎ 04 297 1221; www.southward.org.nz 🕐 Nov–Easter daily 9–5;
Easter–Oct daily 9–4:30 🍴 Tea room ($) 🖐 Inexpensive

MOUNT BRUCE NATIONAL WILDLIFE CENTRE

An important sanctuary for New Zealand's endangered species.
Learn more about kiwi, tuatara and takahe.
www.mtbruce.org.nz
137 E5 ✉ 30km (19 miles) north of Masterton ☎ 06 375 8004
🕐 Daily 9–4:30

MOUNT VICTORIA LOOK-OUT

Rising from Wellington's inner suburbs, this 196m (643ft) peak offers a splendid view of the city and harbour. It is thought to have been used as a look-out point by Maori, who named it Matai-rangi, meaning 'to watch the sky'. Walk or drive to the top.

➕ 144 F4 (off map) 🖐 Inexpensive 🍴 Café Takahe ($) 🚌 2

OTARI–WILTON'S BUSH GARDEN

New Zealand's largest collection of indigenous plants is cultivated here in parkland and gardens. Habitats include native bush, natural forest, an alpine garden and a fernery.

www.owb.co.nz

➕ 144 A1 (off map) ✉ Wilton Road, Wilton ☎ 04 499 1400 🕐 Daily 🖐 Free 🚌 No 14 Wilton bus

THE NEW DOWSE, LOWER HUTT

This exciting gallery is a showcase of New Zealand design, with works ranging from contemporary crafts to paintings and traditional Maori carvings. There is a changing programme of events, including talks and musical performances.

www.dowse.org.nz

➕ 136 E4 ✉ 45 Laings Road ☎ 04 570 6500 🕐 Mon–Fri 10–4:30, Sat–Sun 10–5 🖐 Free 🍴 Reka Café ($$) 🚌 83 🚆 Western Hutt Station

a drive around Wellington

Wellington's Marine Drive starts on Oriental Parade, near the eastern end of Courtenay Place. Note the many narrow and one-way streets in the city centre.

Once on Oriental Parade, continue around Oriental Bay past Mount Victoria (➤ 83).

To drive up Mount Victoria, take Majoribanks Street opposite Courtenay Place then follow signs along the narrow streets to the Admiral Byrd Memorial and Look-out.

Follow Oriental Parade around Point Jerningham into Evans Bay, passing boating facilities and slipways. Turn left onto Cobham Drive, passing the northern end of the airport runway, then keep left out to the next point.

Shelly Bay Road follows the other side of Evans Bay to Point Halswell. Note the Massey Memorial to former Prime Minister William Ferguson Massey (1856–1925).

The route continues past Scorching, Karaka and Worser bays. Continue through Seatoun and the Pass of Branda to rejoin the coast.

Breaker Bay Road follows a bleak stretch of coastline at the harbour entrance. Offshore is Barrett Reef, the craggy rocks where the *Wanganella* ran aground in 1947 and the inter-island ferry *Wahine* foundered in 1968. Moa Point Road leads to the southern end of the airport runway. Continue around Lyall Bay to Island Bay for more views out across Cook Strait.

Return to the city either via Happy Valley and Ohiro and Brooklyn roads to Willis Street and Lambton Quay, or via The Parade and Adelaide Road back to Cambridge Terrace and Courtenay Place.

Distance 40km (25 miles)
Time 2.5 hours
Start/end point Courtenay Place ✚ 144 F4
Lunch Kai in the Bay ($$) ✉ 351 The Parade, Island Bay
☎ 03 383 6442 🕐 Lunch Sat–Sun, dinner Tue–Sun

More to see in the Lower North Island

NAPIER

Hawke's Bay is a picturesque region of hills sweeping down to the central east coast, a fertile plain popularly known as 'the fruit bowl of New Zealand'. It is also a thriving wine producer, with a number of older vineyards. Tragically, the twin cities of Napier and Hastings suffered an earthquake in 1931.

The rebuilding of Napier in the contemporary architecture of the time has made its fascinating art deco design a real attraction, and the traffic-free streets in the town create a pleasant shopping environment.

✚ 137 C6
ℹ 100 Marine Parade ☎ 06 834 1911

Cape Kidnappers

The world's largest known mainland colony of Australasian gannets lies 32km (20 miles) southwest of Napier at the southernmost tip of Hawke's Bay. These large seabirds arrive in July and lay their eggs in October and November; these hatch about six weeks later. The best time to visit the reserve is between November and February.

✚ 137 C6 ✉ Access by tour or on foot (tides permitting) 🖐 Tours moderate; reserve locally

Marine Parade

Attractions along Napier's esplanade include **Hawke's Bay Museum,** which has an interesting audiovisual section on the 1931 earthquake. Other intriguing displays include one devoted to local Maori culture and another to art deco from around the world. At **Marineland,** seals, sea lions, penguins and Kelly the dolphin can all be seen, some in performing shows. Swimming with the dolphins is another option. At the **National Aquarium of New Zealand** is a huge fish tank housing different species of sharks, turtles and

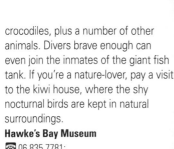

crocodiles, plus a number of other animals. Divers brave enough can even join the inmates of the giant fish tank. If you're a nature-lover, pay a visit to the kiwi house, where the shy nocturnal birds are kept in natural surroundings.

Hawke's Bay Museum
☎ 06 835 7781;
www.hawkesbaymuseum.co.nz ◉ Oct–Apr daily 10–6; May–Sep daily 10–5
✋ Inexpensive

Marineland
☎ 06 834 4027; www.marineland.co.nz
◉ Oct–Apr Tue–Wed, Fri–Sun 10–5:30 Mon, Thu 10–4:30; May–Sep daily 10–4:30
✋ Moderate

National Aquarium of New Zealand
☎ 06 834 1404;
www.nationalaquarium.co.nz
◉ Daily 9–5 ✋ Moderate

Te Mata Peak
A narrow road climbs via Havelock North to the top of this 399m (1,309ft) viewpoint, offering a panorama over the Heretaunga Plains. The peak forms part of the 98ha (242 acre) Te Mata Peak Trust Park, and has good walking routes.
✚ 137 C6 ✉ Te Mata Peak Road; 31km (19 miles) south of Napier
ℹ Havelock North Village Information
☎ 06 877 9600

NEW PLYMOUTH

With the development of oil and gas reserves in the region, the city of New Plymouth, in northern Taranaki, is the 'energy capital'. This is due to the fertile volcanic soils around Mount Taranaki, the region's dominant landmark.

Wellington sits on three major faultlines, one of which ruptured in 1855, causing a massive earthquake measuring 8 on the Richter scale. Although the quake lasted just under a minute, the damage was extensive – the land in the harbour lifted by 1–2m (3–6ft).

www.newplymouthnz.com

✚ 136 B3

ℹ️ Puke Ariki Museum and Library, Ariki Street ☎ 06 759 6080

Govett-Brewster Art Gallery

New Zealand's main contemporary art museum focuses on works by up-and-coming national and Pacific Rim artists. Its collections include work by modernist artist Len Lye (1901–80), whose *Wind Wand* sculpture is on New Plymouth's waterfront.

www.govettbrewster.com

✉️ 42 Queen Street ☎ 06 759 6060 🕐 Oct–Apr daily 10–5; May–Sep daily 10.30–5 🍴 Cafe ($) 🖐️ Free

Mount Taranaki

Visible from New Plymouth and most parts of the Taranaki region, Mount Taranaki, previously known as Mount Egmont, rises 2,518m (8,259ft) in an impressive near-perfect cone from the coastal plain. Captain Cook sighted the volcano in 1770, naming it for the Earl of Egmont, former first Lord of the Admiralty.

The surrounding Egmont National Park has a small winter ski-field and several walking trails. The weather conditions can be unpredictable, but this does not deter the climbers who visit.

✚ 136 C3 🖐️ Free

ℹ️ North Egmont Visitor Centre, Egmont Road ☎ 06 756 0990

🕐 Oct–Apr daily 8–4:30; May–Sep daily 8–4

Pukekura Park

Chief among many parks in New Plymouth, these gardens have fountains, a fernery, woodland and two lakes.

Adjoining Pukekura Park, but separated by a concert bowl, is the more formal Brooklands Park, where there is a rhododendron dell and European-style flower gardens, as well as a small zoo (free).

✉ Fillis Street, New Plymouth 🕐 Nov–Apr daily 7:30–8; Mar–Oct daily 7:30–7 🖐 Free

ℹ Puke Ariki Museum, Ariki Street ☎ 06 759 6080

TONGARIRO NATIONAL PARK

Best places to see, ➤ 28–29.

Upper South Island

Despite being one-third larger in area than the North Island, the South Island has only one-quarter of the country's population. The scenery is internationally renowned for its beauty and variety.

Christchurch

At the top of South Island are three outstanding national parks for visitors to the country to explore: the Abel Tasman National Park, with its beautiful coastline and beaches; and the Kahurangi and Nelson Lakes national parks, characterized by remote bush, mountain scenery and abundant birdlife. To the east are the world-renowned vineyards of Marlborough and the stunning bays of the Marlborough Sounds, while the sea offshore here teems with whales, dolphins and seals.

Christchurch is the South Island's international gateway and also claims the title of its largest city. Considered the most 'English' of New Zealand's cities, it stands on the edge of the Canterbury Plains.

CHRISTCHURCH

Christchurch was founded as a Church of England colony in 1850, and much of its attraction rests with those colonial beginnings, the graceful lines of some of its early neo-Gothic stone buildings contrasting with those of more contemporary design. The city is named after England's Oxford University college, where the city's founding father was educated.

Much of interest lies in the compact downtown area, with the willow-lined Avon River, complete with ducks, ornate bridges, boatsheds and punts, winding around its cathedral and lively central square. Beyond the city centre, numerous parks and gardens grace the flat suburbs, giving Christchurch the nickname of Garden City. To the southeast, the Port Hills separate the city from its port at Lyttelton, while beyond on Banks Peninsula, is New Zealand's only French settlement, Akaroa.

The city makes a good base for exploring. Many long-distance bus tours start and finish here, and options for day trips include whale-watching at Kaikoura (➤ 104–105), swimming at Hanmer's hot springs (➤ 99), taking a train through the Southern Alps, skiing in winter, or visiting Aoraki/Mount Cook, New Zealand's highest mountain (➤ 42–43).

www.christchurchinformation.co.nz

➕ 139 E7 ℹ Old Chief Post Office Building, Cathedral Square ☎ 03 379 9629

Arts Centre

Packed with food and crafts stands, and with live entertainment on weekends, this complex, once part of the university, is equally worth visiting on weekdays. Stores, workshops and galleries sell and display arts and craft works, making it a good place to look for gifts.
www.artscentre.org.nz

✉ 2 Worcester Boulevard ☎ 03 363 2836 ⏰ Daily 10–5
✋ Free 🍴 Four cafés ($) and two restaurants ($$) 🚋 National Christchurch Tramway

Avon River

This stream adds a restful charm to the city as it meanders through Christchurch, and there are walks along its banks. Boats, punts and canoes can be rented – enquire at the **Antigua Boat Sheds.**

The Town Hall complex here includes a concert hall, theatre, conference rooms and restaurant.

Antigua Boat Sheds

✉ 2 Cambridge Terrace ☎ 03 366 5885; www.boatsheds.co.nz
⏰ Oct–Apr daily 9:30–4:30; May–Sep daily 9:30–4
✋ Moderate 🍴 Boatshed Café ($)

Botanic Gardens

The 30ha (74-acre) Botanic Gardens lie within Hagley Park, a vast sports and recreation area on the fringe of the central business district. Set amid the wooded lawns are a number of themed gardens, and there are many displays of flowering trees and exotic plants.

✉ Rolleston Avenue ☎ 03 941 7590; www.ccc.govt.nz/parks (tours) ⏰ Gardens: daily 7am to 1 hour before sunset; conservatories: 10:15–4; guided tours daily 1:30 🍴 Botanic Gardens Café ($); Curator's House Restaurant ($$$)
🚋 Christchurch Tramway

Canterbury Museum

This is a general collection relating to New Zealand history and ethnology. Two specialist exhibits are: The Moa Hunters, with life-size dioramas of early Maori and the giant flightless bird (long extinct); and the excellent Hall of Antarctic Discovery, with relics from the Scott expedition and others. There are free guided tours Tuesdays and Thursdays.

www.canterburymuseum.com

✉ Rolleston Avenue ☎ 03 366 5000 🕐 Oct–Mar daily 9–5:30; Apr–Sep daily 9–5 💲 Free; charges for some exhibits 🍴 Museum Café ($) 🚍 Christchurch Tramway ❓ One-hour free guided tours Tue, Thu

Canterbury Provincial Council Buildings

Built in 1858 beside the Avon River, this Gothic Revival complex reflects the city's English heritage and the early days when New Zealand had 13 independent provinces.

✉ Corner of Durham and Armagh streets ☎ 03 941 7680 🕐 Mon–Sat 10:30–3:30 💲 Free

Christchurch Art Gallery

Opened in this new venue in 2003, the gallery exhibits modern New Zealand and British paintings, as well as a range of other works of art, including ceramics, Maori craft and photography.

✉ Corner of Montreal Street and Worcester Boulevard ☎ 03 941 7300 🕐 Thu–Tue 10–5, Wed 10–9 💲 Free; charges for some exhibitions 🍴 Alchemy Café & Wine Bar ($$$) 🚍 Christchurch Tramway

Christchurch Cathedral

The building of this Gothic Revival edifice, crowned with a 63m (207ft) copper-clad spire, began in 1864 and finished 40 years later.

There are 134 steep steps to the top of the bell tower but the views from the top are worth it.

www.christchurchcathedral.co.nz

✉ Cathedral Square ☎ 03 366 0046 ⏰ Oct–Mar daily 8:30–7; Apr–Sep 9–5. Tower closed until 11:30am Sun ✋ Free; tower inexpensive 🍴 Café ($) 🚋 Christchurch Tramway ❓ Free guided tours Mon–Fri 11, 2, Sat 11, Sun 11:30

Christchurch Tramway

Electric trams first came to Christchurch in 1905 but the network closed in the early 1950s. Now, restored vintage trams take tourists on a scenic route through the city, taking in many of the best sights. Tickets are valid for two days, and passengers can hop on and off to suit.

www.tram.co.nz

✉ From Cathedral Square ☎ 03 366 7830 ⏰ Nov–Mar daily 9–9; Apr–Oct daily 9–6 ✋ Moderate

Science Alive!

In the old Christchurch railway station, this modern interactive science facility offers an educational yet fun-filled experience for people of all ages.

www.sciencealive.co.nz

✉ 392 Moorhouse Avenue ☎ 03 365 5199 ⏰ Sun–Thu 10–5, Fri–Sat 10–6 ✋ Moderate

a walk in Christchurch

Start at the visitor information centre in Cathedral Square, pausing to take a look at the cathedral (➤ 94).

Stroll due west along Worcester Street to the Avon River (➤ 93). The Bridge of Remembrance to the left was built to commemorate Kiwi troops who died during World War I.

After crossing Montreal Street opposite the new Christchurch Art Gallery (➤ 94), pause at the Arts Centre (➤ 93). On weekends, when there are outdoor stalls to browse as well as the many shops, allow extra time. Next, the Canterbury Museum (➤ 94) looms in front.

Continue for two blocks north on Rolleston Avenue, passing Christ's College, and turn east onto Armagh Street. Pass Cranmer Square.

At the Durham Street intersection, note the architecture of the Canterbury Provincial Council Buildings (➤ 94).

Cross the Avon again to enter Victoria Square. Across the square, past statues and fountains, note the award-winning (1972) architecture of the Town Hall.

Turn right from Armagh onto quaint Spanish-style New Regent Street, then head back to Cathedral Square, where there is usually interesting activity.

Distance 2.5km (1.5 miles)
Time 1.5 hours plus stops
Start/end point Cathedral Square
Lunch Annie's Wine Bar & Restaurant ($$)
✉ Arts Centre, 2 Worcester Boulevard ☎ 03 365 0566

Around Christchurch

AKAROA AND BANKS PENINSULA

Within days of the British declaring sovereignty over New Zealand in 1840, a shipload of French settlers founded Akaroa on Banks Peninsula southeast of Christchurch, and it has remained French in spirit ever since.

Mountainous Banks Peninsula is a large volcanic outcrop, with the original craters now forming Lyttelton and Akaroa harbours (➤ 103). Allow time for a cruise.

www.akaroa.com

✚ 139 E7 ✉ SH75; 83km (50 miles) from Christchurch ❚❚ Several restaurants
🚌 Day tours
ℹ Akaroa ☎ 03 304 8600

CHRISTCHURCH GONDOLA

Ride up the side of Mount Cavendish by aerial cable-way from the terminal near the Lyttelton tunnel entrance at Heathcote for a great view over Christchurch and Lyttelton. There is a restaurant, a café, a store and a Time Tunnel display at the upper terminal.

www.gondola.co.nz

✚ 139 E7 ✉ 10 Bridle Path Road, Christchurch ☎ 03 384 0700 🕐 Daily
10–evening 💷 Moderate ❚❚ Summit Café ($$); Pinnacle Restaurant ($$$)
🚌 28, 35

FERRYMEAD HERITAGE PARK

This is a living museum of transport and technology, with a working tramway (weekends), railroad and village, plus displays on household appliances, radios, fire engines and aviation, among others. Hundreds of mechanical musical instruments are another draw. Volunteer groups maintain different portions of the park.
www.ferrymead.org.nz

✚ 139 E7 ✉ 50 Ferrymead Park Drive ☎ 03 384 1970 🕐 Daily 10–4:30
✋ Mon–Fri inexpensive, Sat–Sun moderate 🚌 28, 35

HANMER SPRINGS

Formerly an alpine spa, this outdoor centre 135km (84 miles) north of Christchurch offers skiing in winter and adventure options such as jet-boat rides and bungy-jumping. But the prime attraction is the **Thermal Reserve,** with its hot pools set in landscaped grounds.
✚ 139 D6

Thermal Reserve
✉ Amuri Avenue ☎ 03 315 7511 🕐 Daily 10–9 ✋ Moderate 🍴 Café ($)

INTERNATIONAL ANTARCTIC CENTRE

Located next to the airport and the Operation Deep Freeze base of the United States Air Force, the centre looks at both the geography and the science of the southern polar regions with exhibits and widescreen movies. Some of the highlights are a walk-through polar room (a constant –5°C/23°F), a penguin enclosure and a ride on a Hagglund Antarctic vehicle (additional fee). There is also a souvenir shop and an interactive room.

www.iceberg.co.nz

🕂 139 E7 ⊠ Orchard Road, Harewood, Chirstchurch ☎ 03 353 7798 🕔 Oct–Mar daily 9–7; Apr–Sep daily 9–5:30 💷 Moderate 🍴 Café ($) 🚌 Airport Flyer

LYTTELTON

Canterbury's picturesque port, the largest on the South Island, is reached by road either through a tunnel or over the Port Hills. Take a harbour cruise, then walk around the steep, historic streets to the Timeball Station – the timeball was dropped daily from this castellated structure to signal Greenwich Mean Time to ships in the harbour. The Lyttelton Museum has maritime and colonial displays and an Antarctic gallery.

🕂 139 E7 ⊠ SH74; 13km (8 miles) from Christchurch 🚢 Ferry to Diamond Harbour (Banks Peninsula) daily 🚌 28, 35
🛈 Anchor Fine Arts, 34 London Street
☎ 03 328 9093; www.lytteltonharbour.co.nz

ORANA WILDLIFE PARK

Animals from New Zealand, Africa, Australia, Asia and the Americas can

be seen in this 80ha (200-acre) wildlife park, New Zealand's largest, which specializes in breeding rare and endangered species. There is also a farmyard with domesticated animals, a reptile house, native bird aviaries and a nocturnal kiwi house.
www.oranawildlifepark.co.nz

🟥 139 E7 ✉ McLeans Island Road, Harewood, Christchurch ☎ 03 359 7109
🕐 Daily 10–5 👆 Moderate 🍴 Café ($)

THE TRANZALPINE
Best places to see, ➤ 40–41.

a drive to Akaroa and Banks Peninsula

From Christchurch, the route heads southeast to Banks Peninsula; there are alternatives for the return.

From Cathedral Square, drive south along Colombo Street. After several blocks, turn west (to the right) onto Moorhouse Avenue and follow signs to the left for Akaroa, leading to SH75.

The route leaving the city leads across the coastal plains to Birdlings Flat, skirting Lake Ellesmere, a shallow wetland separated from the sea by the gravelly Kaitorete Spit.

Turn inland to Little River, a former railway terminus.

From here the road climbs steeply up to Hilltop for views over Akaroa Harbour, the crater of an extinct volcano.

The road then drops steeply and follows the harbour round to Akaroa (▶ 98), 83km (51 miles) from Christchurch.

Akaroa's Gallic ancestry is clearly visible in its street names and architecture. In addition to gardens, a museum and a historic lighthouse, a worthwhile attraction is a cruise around the harbour. The *Black Cat* operates daily at 1:30pm (also 11am Nov–Apr) for a two-hour trip, often sighting Hector's dolphins, penguins and seals.

There are alternative return routes to Christchurch, including the high, narrow Summit Road. Either follow the ridge around to Hilltop, or cross over to follow the route round to Lyttelton Harbour. From there, you can return to Christchurch through the tunnel, along the inland Dyers Pass Road, or via the Evans Pass route to Sumner Beach and along the estuary.

Distance 166km (103 miles)
Time Allow a full day
Start/end point Cathedral Square, Christchurch ✚ 139 E7
Lunch Harbour Seventy One ($$$) ✉ 71 Beach Road ☎ 03 304 7656

More to see in the Upper South Island

ABEL TASMAN NATIONAL PARK
Best places to see, ➤ 34–35.

KAHURANGI NATIONAL PARK
Largely mountainous and with very few roads through it, the park is known for the Heaphy Track, an 82km (51-mile) walking route. Forest and bush-clad countryside cover the marble and limestone karst country, which is riddled with extensive cave systems.

✚ 139 B3 ✉ Heaphy Track start/end: 28km (17 miles) southwest of Collingwood ☎ 03 546 8210 (Department of Conservation Nelson) 🕐 Open access to park 🎟 Free 🚌 Shuttle transfers arranged locally

KAIKOURA
This small town on the rocky Kaikoura Coast was formerly a whaling station and is now popular as a whale-watching centre. The main road north and south of the town offers splendid coastal scenery, and the local Maori Leap Cave (2km/1.2 miles south) is famous for its limestone formations.

www.kaikoura.co.nz
🚑 139 B5 ✉ SH1; 184km (114 miles) north of Christchurch 🚌 Daily from Christchurch, Blenheim, Picton 🚆 TranzCoastal daily from Christchurch, Blenheim, Picton
ℹ West End, Kaikoura ☎ 03 319 5641

MARLBOROUGH DISTRICT

The Marlborough district is New Zealand's sunniest region, and as a result the countryside around the town of Blenheim is its premier wine-making region, specializing in sauvignon blanc.

Just outside Blenheim is the **Omaka Aviation Heritage Centre,** which houses one of the world's largest collections of World War I aircraft.

www.destinationmarlborough.com
🚑 139 B7
ℹ Blenheim Railway Station ☎ 03 577 8080

Omaka Aviation Heritage Centre

✉ 93 Aerodrome Road (signed off SH6, 5km/3 miles west of Blenheim)
☎ 03 579 1305; www.omaka.org.nz 🕐 Daily 10–4 💰 Moderate 🍴 Café

NELSON

The sunny city of Nelson sits in the middle of a rich horticultural, forestry and fishing region. It is also noted for its arts and crafts. Foremost among the city's galleries is the **Suter Art Gallery.** The annual Wearable Art Awards may have moved to Wellington, but the weird and wacky fashions are at **WOW,** the World of WearableArt and Classic Cars Museum.

Paths in the Botanical Reserve lead up to a viewpoint known as the Centre of New Zealand. There is excellent swimming at Tahuna Beach and in the nearby Maitai, Aniseed and Lee rivers.

www.nelsonnz.com

🕂 139 B6 ✉ SH6; 438km (272 miles) north of Christchurch

🛈 Taha o te Awa, 77 Trafalgar Street ☎ 03 548 2304

Suter Art Gallery

✉ 208 Bridge Street ☎ 03 548 4699; www.thesuter.org.nz

🕒 Daily 10:30–4:30 🍴 Café ($) ✋ Inexpensive

WOW

✉ 95 Quarantine Road, Annesbrook ☎ 03 547 4573; www.wowcars.co.nz

🕒 10–5 🍴 Café ($) ✋ Moderate

NELSON LAKES NATIONAL PARK

Inland, south of Nelson, the tiny village of St Arnaud is the main gateway to this mountainous park (102,000ha/252,000 acres), known for its twin lakes of Rotoroa and Rotoiti. Alpine St Arnaud village is on the shores of the latter and is popular for boating, fishing and hiking. The small Rainbow Ski Area is also close by.

🕂 139 C6 ✉ Via SH6 and SH63; 119km (74 miles) south of Nelson 🕒 Free access to park 🚌 Bus from Nelson: summer daily; winter Sun, Mon, Wed, Fri

🛈 View Road, St Arnaud ☎ 03 521 1806; www.starnaud.co.nz

PICTON AND THE MARLBOROUGH SOUNDS

Picton, at the head of Queen Charlotte Sound, is the commercial focus for the sea inlets formed from the drowned valleys known as

the Marlborough Sounds. In a covered dry dock is the hulk of the 1853 clipper ship *Edwin Fox*, a former carrier of tea, troops, convicts, meat and coal; it is currently being restored. Picton Museum also has an interesting local collection to see.

Launch cruises and fishing trips can be taken around the sounds and there are also walking trails, some requiring several days to complete. There is lodge accommodation on some of the walks, including the renowned Queen Charlotte Track.

www.destinationmarlborough.com

➕ Picton: 139 A7; Marlborough Sounds: 135 A7 ✉ SH1; 28km (17.5 miles) north of Blenheim 🚢 From Wellington

ℹ The Foreshore, Picton ☎ 03 520 3113

Lower South Island

The lower half of South Island is home to some of New Zealand's most spectacular scenery. Flowing west out of the snowfields of the Southern Alps are the Fox and Franz Josef glaciers, while to the south, beyond more dramatic peaks, is Fiordland. This region of steep-sided inlets and remote forests and lakes is one of the world's largest and most impressive national parks.

Dunedin

Lovers of the great outdoors are always attracted to photogenic Queenstown, on Lake Wakatipu. Within easy reach of fjords and a

centre for skiing and various adventure options for serious thrill-seekers, it is a world-famous holiday destination, and rightly so. South is Invercargill, regional hub of Southland and the main departure point for New Zealand's often forgotten third island, Stewart Island. This island is a true haven for bush wildlife and offers the chance to see animals in their natural environment. The region's other main city is Dunedin. This lively city is renowned for its proud Scottish heritage and for its university.

QUEENSTOWN

The South Island's second largest lake, Wakatipu, with the Remarkables mountain range as a backdrop, provides a dramatic and picturesque setting for Queenstown on its northeastern shore.

This is undoubtedly New Zealand's premier resort for adventure and action, offering a host of exhilarating activities ranging from jet-boating on the nearby Shotover and Kawarau rivers to helicopter trips over the mountains, from bungy-jumping to skiing at Coronet Peak, and from paragliding to white-water rafting.

Less sensational but equally appealing are the gentler pursuits of lake cruising on an old steamboat, hiking, horseback riding and fishing. For those who prefer just to look, there are museums, parks and gardens around the town. Not to be missed is the Skyline Gondola (➤ 38) for spectacular views of the lake.

The nightlife here is just as lively, and there are many bars, cafés and restaurants and a good range of entertainment. Shoppers and strollers are well catered to, with Church Street and the Mall running down to the waterfront, the focal point of the town.

Formerly a gold-mining town, Queenstown has come to rely on tourism since the beginning of the last century and now makes every possible effort to attract visitors from around the world.
www.queenstown-vacation.com

✚ 140 C3

ℹ Clocktower Building, corner of Shotover and Camp streets ☎ 03 442 4100

TSS *Earnslaw*
The lake steamer TSS *Earnslaw*, built in 1912, operates frequent cruises from its wharf near downtown. This 'lady of the lake' offers local sightseeing trips and excursions to Walter Peak Farm, a high-country sheep station across the lake where sheep-shearing and dog-handling are demonstrated.

✉ Steamer Wharf ☎ 03 442 7500; www.realjourneys.co.nz

🕐 Oct to mid-Apr daily 10, 12, 2, 4, 6, 8; mid-Apr to Sep daily 12, 2, 4

✋ Expensive 🍴 On-board café ($); 6pm summer cruise can include dinner at Walter Peak ($$$)

Flight Experience
Remain safe while having your thrills on this flight simulator ride. Fly the Boeing 737 from Christchurch to Queenstown, or attempt a landing at Hong Kong's notoriously difficult Kai Tak Airport.
www.flightexperience.co.nz

✉ Crowne Plaza, Beach Street ☎ 03 442 8878 🕐 Daily 9–9 ✋ Expensive

Kiwi Birdlife Park
A number of aviaries, including some housing endangered species, a native bush area, a nocturnal kiwi house and a replica Maori hunting village are the main attractions here.
www.kiwibird.co.nz

✉ Brecon Street ☎ 03 442 8059 🕐 Oct–Apr daily 9–7; May–Sep daily 9–5 (times may vary) ✋ Moderate 🍴 Dinner plus evening tour available ($$$)

Queenstown Gardens

Queenstown Gardens, with trees and shrubs,
flower gardens, and recreational areas, cover a
small promontory jutting into the lake. They were
established in 1867. On the short walk along the
beach from downtown, there are views of the
mountains through the trees.

Williams Cottage, at the entrance to the Gardens,
dates from 1865 and is one of Queenstown's oldest
buildings.

✉ Marine Parade or Park Street ◷ Unrestricted access

Skyline Gondola

Best places to see, ➤ 38–39.

Underwater World

At the end of the main pier on Queenstown's
waterfront is this below-lake observatory. Through
the huge windows interested spectators can view
the lake's inhabitants at close quarters, including
trout, eels and scaup (diving ducks).

✉ Rees Street ☎ 03 442 6142 ◷ Daily 9–5 💰 Inexpensive

Around Queenstown

ARROWTOWN

With its stone cottages and exotic trees such as
sycamore and oak, this attractive old gold-mining
town is less commercialized than Queenstown. The
main shopping street is lovely to stroll along, and a
visit to the Lakes District Museum and Gallery is
particularly informative.

The return trip to Queenstown via Lake Hayes is
especially beautiful in the autumn.

✚ 140 C3 ✉ 20km (12.5 miles) from Queenstown
🛈 Clocktower Building, corner of Shotover and Camp
streets ☎ 03 442 4100

CORONET PEAK

Between June and October this is one of
the region's leading ski fields, but it is worth
visiting at any time of the year as the 18km
(11-mile) drive offers sky-high views over
Lake Wakatipu and the surrounding
countryside. During the skiing season a
regular bus shuttle operates.
www.nzski.com/coronet
✚ 140 C3 ✉ 18km (11 miles) from Queenstown
☎ 03 442 46400 (Queenstown Snow Centre)
🍽 Winter only 🚌 Shuttle in ski season

SKIPPERS CANYON

The narrow cliffside road leading 17km (10
miles) to the remnants of Skippers, a former
gold-mining township, is the main attraction
here, but only experienced drivers should
attempt it (rental vehicles are prohibited).
  Various adventure activities take place above
and along the river, if you're brave enough. The
Shotover Canyon Swing involves launching
yourself into the canyon from a height of 109m
(358ft), while the Shotover Jet is a thrilling
speed-boat ride that twists around the river's
rocky walls. Another adrenaline-pumped water-
based option is white-water rafting.
✚ 140 C3 ✉ 28km (17.5 miles) from Queenstown
❓ Tours of the canyon are available (expensive)
🛈 Clocktower Building, Queenstown ☎ 03 442 4100

a walk in Queenstown

The first part of this stroll around Queenstown is flat, but the second part involves a climb in the countryside.

From the wharf at the foot of the Mall, outside Eichardt's Hotel, walk towards the peninsula jutting into the lake. This short stroll, either along the lake's beach or adjacent footpath, leads to the Queenstown Gardens (➤ 112).

Here, paths lead past flowers and trees, as well as recreational amenities such as tennis courts and a bowling rink. There are views back through the trees to downtown Queenstown or out over the lake. The impressive southeastward view across the lake includes the Remarkables range.

Loop around to the access road (Park Street) and walk up the streets behind Queenstown. Turn left at the top of Sydney Street onto Hallenstein Street, then right onto Edgar and Kent streets.

From here, note the signposted Queenstown Hill Walkway. Follow this path for some 4.5km (2.5 miles), ascending to a height of about 900m (3,000ft). The path passes through bush (mostly exotic trees, including pine and fir), with the vegetation becoming scrubbier at higher altitudes. There are patches of schist rock and a small tarn (lake) on the way. The splendid view opens out over the town, Lake Wakatipu and surrounding mountains to reveal the steep glaciated valleys and mountainsides of the area.

Return by the same route.

Distance 10km (6 miles)
Time 3.5 hours
Start/end point Foot of the Mall ✚ 140 C3
Lunch The Bathhouse ($$$) ✉ 15–28 Marine Parade ☎ 03 442 5625

More to see in the Lower South Island

AORAKI/MOUNT COOK NATIONAL PARK
Best places to see, ► 42–43

BLUFF
Invercargill's port of Bluff lies below Bluff Hill at the tip of the South Island. A road leads up to a look-out with views across the harbour to Stewart Island (► 126). SH1 terminates at land's end at Stirling Point, with its much-photographed signpost .
www.bluff.co.nz

✚ 140 E4 ✉ SH1; 27km (16.5 miles) south of Invercargill
🛈 108 Gala Street, Invercargill ☎ 03 214 6243

CATLINS
This coastal strip at the southeast corner of the South Island has a spectacular coastline of rugged, lonely beaches, while inland lie tracts of undisturbed forests supporting plant and animal species.
www.catlins.org.nz

✚ 141 E5 ✉ 138km (85.5 miles) east of Invercargill
🛈 Owaka ☎ 03 415 8371

CROMWELL
East of Queenstown, in the barren landscape of central Otago, Cromwell was partly rebuilt in the 1980s when the Clutha River was dammed to form Lake Dunstan. The story of the Clyde Dam, and of Cromwell's origins as a gold-mining settlement, is presented in the town's information centre and museum.
www.cromwell.org.nz

✚ 140 C4 ✉ SH6 and SH8; 57km (35.5 miles) from Wanaka 🚌 Scheduled coach service daily from Franz Josef, Christchurch, Queenstown and Dunedin
🛈 47 The Mall, Cromwell ☎ 03 445 0212

DUNEDIN

The town was founded in 1848 by settlers of the Free Church of Scotland at the head of Otago Harbour, a long waterway sheltered by the scenic Otago Peninsula (➤ 126).

Prosperity soon followed in the wake of the 1860s Otago gold rush, and the city became New Zealand's wealthiest, leaving a legacy of handsome, well-preserved buildings. Above all though, Dunedin is known as a university city (New Zealand's first university was founded here in 1869), with a lively social, arts and music scene.

The Octagon, at the heart of the town, is dominated by a statue to the Scottish poet Robert Burns and the imposing Anglican St Paul's Cathedral. The fact that the country's only whisky distillery was located in Dunedin is another reminder of its Scottish connections.

The extensive botanic gardens (the first to be created in New Zealand, in 1863) at the northern end of the city include a rose garden, an aviary, a rhododendron dell (best seen between October and November when in bloom), azalea beds and winter gardens.

www.cityofdunedin.com

✚ 141 C6

🛈 48 The Octagon ☎ 03 474 3300

Hocken Library

The library houses a collection of historic books, early manuscripts, paintings and photographs relating to Otago and the Pacific. General browsing of shelves is not permitted.

✉ Corner of Anzac Avenue and Parry Street
☎ 03 479 8868 🕔 Mon, Wed–Fri 9:30–5, Tue 9:30–5, 6–9, Sat 9–12 ✋ Free ❓ Tours Wed 11, 2

Olveston House

This stone Jacobean-style mansion, built at the start of the 20th century, illustrates the lifestyle of its wealthy owners, the Theomin family. Most of the well-preserved contents of the house, including a collection of paintings, were gathered during the family's extensive travels overseas.
www.olveston.co.nz
✉ 42 Royal Terrace ☎ 03 477 3320 🕔 Set tours daily: 9:30, 10:45, 12, 1:30, 2:45 and 4 (reservations essential) ✋ Moderate

Otago Museum

Noted for its Maori and Pacific Island sections, the museum also has a comprehensive natural history section, a maritime exhibition and several decorative arts items from Asia. Discovery World has many scientific hands-on exhibits.
www.otagomuseum.govt.nz
✉ 419 Great King Street ☎ 03 474 7474 🕔 Daily 10–5 ✋ Free; Discovery World inexpensive

EXPLORING

Otago Settlers Museum
This museum tells the story of Otago's social history and includes sections on early Maori habitation and Chinese settlement during the gold-rush era. There is also a photographic gallery of early settler portraits, displayed with furniture and objects from the era. Also housed here is New Zealand's oldest existing steam locomotive (1872).

www.otago.settlers.museum

✉ 31 Queens Gardens ☎ 03 477 5052
🕐 Daily 10–5 🎫 Free

Signal Hill
Located in suburban Opoho, this 393m (1,289ft) peak offers a panorama over central Dunedin. A viewing terrace erected in 1940 marks the centenary of British sovereignty in New Zealand.

✉ End of Signal Hill Road 🕐 Unrestricted access

Taieri Gorge Railway
The four-hour return trip to Pukerangi along the craggy Taieri Gorge aboard a diesel-hauled excursion train leaves Dunedin station every day. In addition to the scenery, there are many Victorian bridges and viaducts to admire. Dunedin Railway Station, a grand Edwardian (1906) building with an ornate interior, is a landmark.

www.taieri.co.nn

✉ Dunedin Railway Station ☎ 03 477 4449 🕐 Oct–Apr daily 2:30; Mar–Sep daily 12:30 🎫 Expensive 🍴 Refreshments on train ($)

FIORDLAND NATIONAL PARK
Best places to see, ► 26–27.

FOX AND FRANZ JOSEF GLACIERS

These two huge glaciers, situated some 25km (16 miles) apart, are the main draws of Westland National Park. They are the only glaciers that descend as low as 300m (1,000ft) above sea level in temperate zones. Guided tours and hikes, including helicopter trips, are available from Fox and Franz Josef villages, which have visitor centres. The national park headquarters, which includes a display about the glaciers, is at Franz Josef.

www.glaciercountry.co.nz

✚ 138 F4 ✉ Glaciers: SH6; 187km (116 miles) from Greymouth

🛈 Fox Glacier visitor information ☎ 03 751 0807

🛈 Franz Josef Glacier visitor information ☎ 03 752 0796

HAAST

Situated 117km (72 miles) south of Fox Glacier, this settlement marks the entrance to the Haast Pass route. Centred on the UNESCO-designated Southwest New Zealand World Heritage Area, the Haast region includes the country's most extensive area of wetlands, rainforests, coastal lagoons and swamps.

✛ 140 A3 ✉ SH6; 317km (197 miles) southwest of Greymouth 🚌 Daily from the glaciers and Queenstown

ℹ Haast visitor centre ☎ 03 750 0809 🕓 Daily 8:30–4

INVERCARGILL

New Zealand's southernmost city lies in a flat pastoral region close to Foveaux Strait. Its main attraction is the **Southland Museum and Art Gallery** in Queens Park, with displays about natural history, colonial settlers and Maori heritage. Two more attractions are an enclosure housing living specimens of the rare tuatara, and a presentation about the sub-Antarctic islands – five uninhabited rocky clusters lying up to 700km (430 miles) to the south.

www.visitinvercargillnz.com

✛ 140 E4

ℹ 108 Gala Street ☎ 03 214 6243

Southland Museum and Art Gallery

✉ Gala Street, Queens Park ☎ 03 219 9069; www.southlandmuseum.com

🕓 Mon–Fri 9–5, Sat–Sun 10–5 🖐 Free 🍴 Café ($)

LAKE MANAPOURI AND DOUBTFUL SOUND

The best way to enjoy the beauty of this lake is by taking a cruise. The most popular trip is to West Arm, where an underground hydroelectric power plant has been built. Access to the powerhouse is by coach along a 2km (1-mile) tunnel. Some tours continue across the Wilmot Pass to the remote sea inlet of Doubtful Sound, where another cruise can be taken.

✛ Lake Manapouri: 140 D3; Doubtful Sound: 140 D2 ✉ South of Te Anau

☎ 03 249 6602 (Real Journeys); www.realjourneys.co.nz 🕓 West Arm: daily

12:30. Doubtful Sound (day): Oct–Apr daily 9:30; May–Sep daily 9:45. Doubtful Sound (overnight): Nov–Apr daily 12:30; May daily 12

LAKE TEKAPO

Accessible from the main road between Christchurch and Mount Cook Village, the lake lies at the northern end of the Mackenzie Country basin. Glacial deposits account for the amazing milky turquoise colour of the water.

A picturesque stone chapel on the edge of the lake, built in 1935, is a favourite tourist stop. Alpine flights are also available.

✚ 139 F5 ✉ SH8; 226km (140 miles) southwest of Christchurch 🚌 Daily from Christchurch and Queenstown ℹ 03 680 6686

MILFORD SOUND

Best places to see, ➤ 26–27.

a drive from Queenstown to Milford Sound

Whether undertaken by rental car or coach, the most popular road tour from Queenstown is the round trip to Milford Sound (➤ 26). Allowing time for a cruise on the fjord, it is a 12-hour day.

From Queenstown, drive 7km (4 miles) round to Frankton on SH6A to join SH6, southbound.

The road winds around the bluffs above Lake Wakatipu, passing Kingston at its southern end before rising over a crest to enter farmland.

The road leads to Lumsden to pick up SH94 west, but follow the signposted short cut via SH97 at Five Rivers.

From Mossburn, the road crosses progressively more barren countryside. Note a loop road to Manapouri before arriving at Te Anau (➤ 127).

From Te Anau, SH94 turns northwards, then runs parallel with Lake Te Anau and enters the beech forest of the Eglinton Valley. As the mountains close in, the Divide is crossed into the upper Hollyford Valley and the road climbs up to the Homer Tunnel. On emerging, the road zigzags down to Milford Sound, where a hotel, an airstrip and other facilities have been built. The road ends here. The return is via the same route, although tours also offer coach/fly options.

A cruise on the fjord, with its high, steep sides and waterfalls, is recommended. The facilities at Milford are limited, but basic accommodation and a café are available.

In winter (June to August) the road is prone to snow and there is a risk of avalanches (call 0900 33 222 to check).

Distance 291km (180 miles) each way
Time A 12-hour day with stops
Start/end point Downtown Queenstown ✚ 140 C3
Lunch Blue Duck Bar and Café ($$) ✉ Milford Sound
☎ 03 249 7931

MILFORD TRACK

Often described as 'the finest walk in the world', this four-day, 54km (34-mile) hike runs from the top of Lake Te Anau to Milford Sound. Boat access is required at both ends, and walkers can choose either to travel independently, overnighting in park huts, or join a fully guided trip. Both options require advance reservations.

✚ 140 C2 ☎ 03 249 8514 for reservations; www.doc.govt.nz 🖐 Expensive

OTAGO PENINSULA

The craggy peninsula guarding Dunedin's harbour is renowned for its wildlife. It's also home to **Larnach Castle,** built in 1871, complete with ballroom and battlements. The castle has been renovated and is open to view and offers limited accommodation. Glenfalloch Woodland Garden is also popular (inexpensive).

There are several wildlife reserves on the peninsula, but the most special is the **Royal Albatross Centre** at Taiaroa Head, the only mainland breeding colony for giant royal albatrosses in the southern hemisphere. The colony has a special viewing gallery.

✚ 141 C6

Larnach Castle

✉ Camp Road ☎ 03 476 1616;
www.larnachcastle.co.nz ⏰ Daily 9–5
🖐 Moderate 🍴 Café ($)

Royal Albatross Centre

✉ Harrington Point Road ☎ 03 478 0499
(reservations essential);
www.albatross.org.nz ⏰ Oct–Apr daily
9–dusk; May–Nov Wed–Mon 10–4, Tue
10:30–4. Viewing observatory closed 17
Sep–23 Nov 🖐 Moderate 🍴 Café ($–$$)

STEWART ISLAND AND RAKIURA NATIONAL PARK

New Zealand's third largest island, covering 1,746sq km (674sq miles), lies 27km (16.5 miles) south of the South Island. It can be

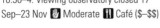

reached by air from Invercargill or by catamaran from Bluff. Although there are few roads, there are good walking trails, including the arduous 10-day North-West Circuit.
www.stewartisland.co.nz

🚉 140 F4 🚢 Foveaux Express catamaran (☎ 03 212 7660; www.stewartislandexperience.co.nz) ✈ Stewart Island Flights (☎ 03 218 9129; www.stewartislandflights.com)

ℹ Elgin Terrace, Halfmoon Bay, Stewart Island ☎ 03 219 1400

TE ANAU

Gateway to Fiordland National Park (➤ 26–27), the township beside Lake Te Anau is the main centre for the area and the starting point for many walking trails and boat cruises. One of the latter takes visitors to the **Te Anau Glowworm Caves,** where there is a glow-worm grotto. At the Te Anau Wildlife Centre you can see the takahe, a flightless bird believed to be extinct until 1948.

🚉 140 D3

ℹ Lakefront Drive, Te Anau ☎ 03 249 8900; www.fiordland.org.nz

Te Anau Glowworm Caves

✉ Real Journeys, Lakefront Drive ☎ 03 249 7416; www.realjourneys.co.nz
🕐 Oct–Apr daily 2, 5:45, 7, 8:15; May–Sep daily 2, 7 💷 Expensive

TWIZEL AND LAKE PUKAKI

The road from Twizel to Mount Cook Village (➤ 43) runs alongside the glacier-fed Lake Pukaki, known for its distinctive blue colouring. Built in 1968 as a service town for the Upper Waitaki hydroelectricity scheme, it now serves the tourist industry.

✚ 140 A4 ✉ SH8; 284km (176 miles) southwest of Christchurch 🚌 Daily from Christchurch and Queenstown
ℹ️ Twizel Events Centre
☎ 03 435 3124; www.twizel.com

WANAKA

Forming the eastern gateway to South Westland via the Haast Pass, Wanaka is on the shores of Lake Wanaka. The town has skiing in season and is the main base for Mount Aspiring National Park. In town are mazes and illusions at **Puzzling World**. The **New Zealand Fighter Pilots Museum** hosts the large biennial Warbirds Over Wanaka airshow.

✚ 140 B4 ℹ️ The Log Cabin, Lakefront, 100 Ardmore Street, Wanaka
☎ 03 443 1233; www.lakewanaka.co.nz;
ℹ️ Mount Aspiring National Park Centre: 03 443 7660

Puzzling World

✉ SH84 (main Queenstown road) ☎ 03 443 7489; www.puzzlingworld.co.nz
🕐 Oct–Apr daily 8:30–5:30; May–Sep daily 8:30–5 🍴 Café ($), separate from attractions 💲 Inexpensive

New Zealand Fighter Pilots Museum

✉ Wanaka Airport, SH6 ☎ 03 443 7010; www.nzfpm.co.nz 🕐 Daily 9–4
💲 Inexpensive; Warbirds Over Wanaka: expensive

WESTLAND NATIONAL PARK

Exploring, ➤ 121, Fox and Franz Josef glaciers.

WHITE HERON SANCTUARY

Amid the lagoons that lie on the northern fringes of Westland National Park is New Zealand's only breeding site for the white heron. These majestic birds nest between October and March, during which time tours may be taken to see them. Tours leave from Whataroa, and include a jet-boat ride, a ride in a minivan and a short walk.

🔟 138 E4 ✉ Whataroa; 140km (87 miles) south of Greymouth

☎ Tours: 03 753 4120; www.whiteherontours.co.nz ♿ Access controlled

💰 Expensive 🚌 Daily from Greymouth, Nelson, and the glaciers

Index

Acknowledgements

The Automobile Association would like to thank the following photographers, companies and picture libraries for their assistance in the preparation of this book.

Abbreviations for the picture credits are as follows: (t) top; (b) bottom; (l) left; (r) right; (AA) AA World Travel Library.

4l Abel Tasman National Park water taxi, AA/M Langford; **4c** Hooker Valley, AA/M Langford; **4r** Seaward Kaikoura Range, AA/P Kenward; **5l** Lower Shotover Gorge jet boat, AA/A Reisinger & V Meduna; **5c** Akaroa Heritage Path, AA/A Belcher; **6/7** Milford Sound, AA/P Kenward; **8/9** Auckland, AA/A Belcher; **10/11** Abel Tasman National Park water taxi, AA/M Langford; **14/15** Tauranga Jazz Festival, AA/M Langford; **17** Bus stop sign, AA/M Langford; **18t** Auckland taxi, AA/M Langford; **18b** Penguin crossing sign, AA/ P Kenward; **19** Auckland bank ATM, AA/M Langford; **20** Auckland public telephone, AA/M Langford; **21** Policeman, AA/A Belcher; **24/25** Hooker Valley, AA/M Langford; **26** Bowen Falls, AA/A Belcher; **26/27** Milford Sound, AA/P Kenward; **28** Mount Ngauruhoe, AA/M Langford; **28/29** Tongariro National Park, AA/P Kenward; **30/31** Te Papa Museum, AA/A Belcher; **31** Museum of New Zealand, AA/P Kenward; **32** Whakarewarewa, Maori children, AA/A Belcher; **32/33** Whakarewarewa Thermal Reserve, AA/M Langford; **33** Whakarewarewa, AA/A Belcher; **34** Abel Tasman National Park water taxi, AA/M Langford; **34/35** Abel Tasman National Park, AA/P Kenward; **35** Cormorant, AA/M Langford; **36/37** Ninety Mile Beach, AA/P Kenward; **38/39** Queenstown and Lake Wakatipu, AA/P Kenward; **40** Trans Alpine Express, AA/A Belcher; **40/41** Arthur's Pass, AA/A Belcher; **42** Hooker Valley Lily, AA/M Langford; **42/43** Hooker Valley, AA/M Langford; **43** Tasman Glacier, AA/M Langford; **44/45t** Aranui Cave, AA/M Langford; **44/45b** Mangapohue Natural Bridge, AA/M Langford; **46/47** Seaward Kaikoura Range, AA/P Kenward; **49** Sky Tower, AA/M Langford; **50** Fountain in Albert Park, AA/A Belcher; **50/51** Albert Park from Sky Tower, AA/A Belcher; **52/53** View from North Head, AA/M Langford; **54/55** Auckland Harbour Bridge, AA/A Belcher; **55** Kelly Tarlton's Underwater World and Antarctic Encounter, AA/P Kenward; **56/57t** Auckland to Rangitoto Island, AA/M Langford; **56/57b** Museum of Transport and Technology, AA/P Kenward; **57** Auckland Maritime Museum, AA/A Belcher; **58/59** Auckland Botanic Gardens, AA/M Langford; **59** Waitakere Rangers, AA/M Langford; **60** Parnell Village Shops signs, AA/P Kenward; **60/61** Ferry Building, AA/M Langford; **62** Kerikeri Stone Store, AA/A Belcher; **62/63** Kerikeri inlet, AA/A Belcher; **64/65** Waitangi National Reserve Meeting House, AA/A Belcher; **66** Maori Warrior, AA/P Kenward; **67** Hell's Gate Thermal Reserve, AA/M Langford; **68** Maori St Faith's Anglican Church Ohinemutu, AA/P Kenward; **68/69** Rainbow Springs, AA/P Kenward; **70** Waimangu Volcanic Valley, AA/M Langford; **70/71** Champagne Pool Wai O Tapu Thermal Area, AA/M Langford; **72** Huka Falls, AA/P Kenward; **73** Taupo rock carvings, AA/A Belcher; **74** Wellington harbour, AA/A Belcher; **75** Around Napier, AA/P Kenward; **76** Museum of New Zealand, AA/P Kenward; **77** Wellington Zoo flowers, AA/P Kenward; **78/79t** Old St Paul's Cathedral, AA/P Kenward; **78/79b** Parliament Building, AA/A Belcher; **80/81** Kapiti Coast, AA/M Langford; **82** Mount Bruce National Wildlife Centre, AA/P Kenward; **82/83** Mount Victoria, AA/A Belcher; **84/85** Oriental Bay fountain, AA/M Langford; **86/87t** Napier, AA/P Kenward; **86/87c** Cape Kidnappers Gannets, AA/P Kenward; **87** Hawke's Bay, AA/M Langford; **88/89** Pukakura Park, AA/P Kenward; **90** Lyttelton, AA/A Belcher; **91** Christchurch, AA/M Langford; **92/93** Christchurch River Avon, AA/M Langford; **94** Canterbury Museum, AA/P Kenward; **94/95** Christchurch tram, AA/M Langford; **97** Statue and Christchurch Cathedral, AA/M Langford; **98** Akaroa Tawhiri Makea statue, AA/A Belcher; **99** Hanmer Springs, AA/P Kenward; **100/101** Lyttelton, AA/A Belcher; **102** Banks Peninsula, AA/A Belcher; **103** Summit Road, AA/M Langford; **104/105** Kaikoura Bay sperm whale, AA/P Kenward; **106** Trafalgar Street Nelson, AA/M Langford; **106/107** Edwin Fox Picton, AA/M Langford; **107** Queen Charlotte Sound, AA/M Langford; **108** Lower Shotover Gorge jet boat, AA/A Reisinger & V Meduna; **109** Doubtful Sound, AA/M Langford; **110/111** Steamer Wharf Village, AA/P Kenward; **112/113** Arrowtown War Memorial, AA/A belcher; **114/115** Queenstown Botanical Gardens, AA/P Kenward; **116** Bluff signpost, AA/M Langford; **116/117** Old Cromwell Town, AA/M Langford; **117** Cromwell sculpture, AA/P Kenward; **118/119** Dunedin Octagon, AA/P Kenward; **119** Dunedin Burns statue, AA/A Belcher; **120** Dunedin Settlers Museum, AA/N Hanna; **120/121** Taiere Gorge Train, AA/A Belcher; **121** Dunedin Railway Station, AA/P Kenward; **122/123** Lake Manapouri Te Anau, AA/P Kenward; **123** Lake Tekapo, AA/M Langford; **124/125** Mitre Peak, AA/P Kenward; **126** Royal Albatros, AA/P Kenward; **126/127** Oban Wharf Stewart Island, AA/M Langford; **128/129** Californian Poppies, Wanaka, AA/M Langford

Every effort has been made to trace the copyright holders, and we apologize in advance for any accidental errors. We would be happy to apply the corrections in the following edition of this publication.

Maps

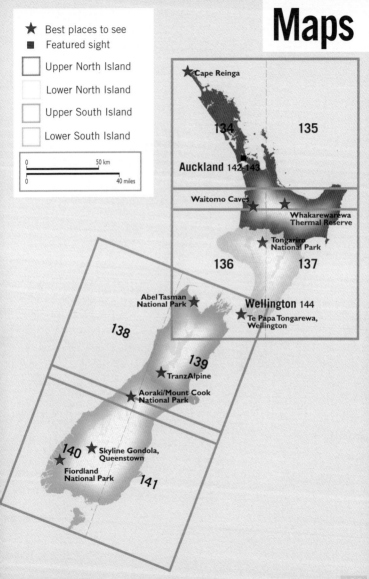

★ Best places to see
■ Featured sight
☐ Upper North Island
☐ Lower North Island
☐ Upper South Island
☐ Lower South Island

0   50 km
0   40 miles

★ Cape Reinga

134   135

■ Auckland 142–143

Waitomo Caves ★   ★ Whakarewarewa Thermal Reserve

★ Tongariro National Park

136   137

Abel Tasman National Park ★

138

Wellington 144
★ Te Papa Tongarewa, Wellington

139
★ TranzAlpine

★ Aoraki/Mount Cook National Park

140 ★ Skyline Gondola, Queenstown

★ Fiordland National Park

141

	1	2	3	4
A				
B				
C				
D				
E				
F				

Cape Reinga
Spirits Bay
Kapowairua
Cape Maria Van Diemen
North Cape
Te Paki
Paua
Great Exhibition Bay
Te Kao
Ngataki
Karikari Peninsula
Ninety Mile Beach
Aupouri Peninsula
Hukatere
Rangaunu Bay
Doubtless Bay
Cavalli Islands
Waipapakauri Beach
Ahipara Bay
315m
Taipa
Taupo Bay
Matauri Bay
Bay of Islands Maritime and Historic Park
Ahipara
Kaitaia
Kaeo
Te Tii
Cape Brett
Tauroa Point
Mangapa
Kerikeri
Awaroa
Mangamuka
Puketi
Bay of Islands
Rawhiti
Waitangi Historic Reserve
Russell
Whangape
Ranglahua
Paihia
Pakaraka
608m
Rawene
Kaikohe
407m
Whangaruru Harbour
Poor Knights Islands Marine Reserve
Mitimiti
12
Taheke
Helena Bay
Omapere
NORTHLAND
Mataraua
Whananaki
Waimamaku
Waipoua Kauri Forest
575m
Otakairangi
Whakapara
Twin Bridges
Tutukaka Coast
Katui
770m
Ngunguru
Kaihu
Jutamoe
Whangarei
Pataua North
Omamari
Pukehuia
Oakleigh
Ocean Beach
Dargaville
Kaiiwi Lake
Ruakaka
Hen and Chickens Islands
Baylys Beach
Ruarangi
Bream Bay
Mititai
Waipu
270m
Paparoa
Brynderwyn
Motairehe
Ruawai
12
Jellicoe Channel
Little Barrier Island
Taingaehe
Hukatere
Te Arai
Rototuna
Port Albert
Goat Island Marine Reserve
Colville
Oneriri
Wellsford
Pouto
Tapora
Kawau Bay
Hauraki Islands
Port Jackson
North Head
Tauhoa
Warkworth
Kawau Marine Park
South Head
106m
Puhoi
Hauraki Gulf Marine Park
Coromandel Forest Park
South Head
Araparera
Orewa
Hauraki Gulf
Colville
Shelly Beach
Kaukapakapa
Dairy Flat
Whangaparaoa
Wharepapa
Albany
Waiheke Island
Coromandel
Kumeu
Onetoa
Ponui Island
Muriwai Beach
AUCKLAND
Kereta
Te Henga
Waiatarua
Maraetai
Orere Point
Piha
Auckland Botanic Gardens
Waitakere Ranges Regional Park
Whatipu
Papakura
Firth of Thames
Awhitu
Manukau Harbour
Runciman
Kaiaua
Clarks Beach
Pukekohe
Waitakaruru
Waiuku
Pokeno
Otaua
Tuakau
Okaeria
Port Waikato
Glen Murray
Kaihere
Lake Waikare
Limestone Downs
Ohinewai
Waikorea
Lake Whangape
Huntly
Te Akau
Ngaruawahia
Morrinsville
Raglan
756m Mt Karioi
Te Mata
HAMILTON
Rahanui
Ohaupo
Te Awamutu
Kawhia
959m Mt Pirongia (31)
Tihiroa
Kawhia Harbour
Taharoa
Te Anga
Waitomo Caves
Otorohanga
Kiritehere
Te Kuiti

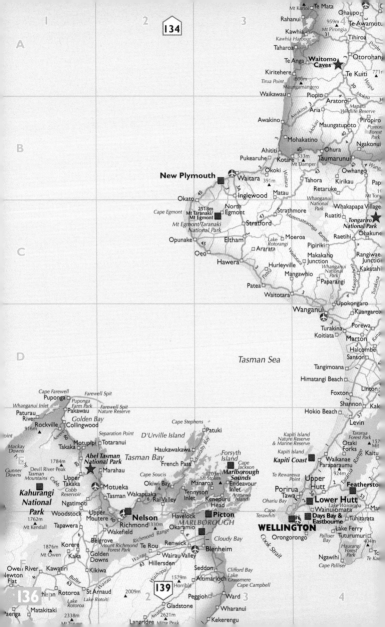

	1	2	3	4
A				Kahura
B				Karamea *Bight*
C				Westpo *Cape Foulwind* *Tauranga Bay* *Nine Mile* *Beach* Charleston Tiromoana Punakaiki *Perpendicular Point* Barrytow
D				Runan Greymouth Paro Kumara Junctio Awatuna Hokitika Ruatapu
E				Ro Pukekura *Lake* *Ianthe* Waita Hariharim *Wan* **White Heron** **Sanctuary** *Okarito Lagoon* Okarito
F				*Lake* *Mapourika* Whataroa *Westland /* *Tai Poutini* *Franz Josef* *National Park* *Glacier* *Fox Glacier* *Aoraki /* Gillespies Beach Fox *Mount Cook* Glacier *National Pa* Karangarua 3754m ▲ *Westland /* *Aoraki* *Tai Poutini* *Mt Cook* Jacobs River 3157m ▲ *Bruce Bay* Mt Sefton Mahitahi 3151m ▲ Mount Cook Village

Knights Point □Lake Paringa
2652m ▲
Lake Moeraki Mount Hooker

National Park
Jacobs River
Bruce Bay
Mahitahi
Mt Sefton 3157m
Mount Cook
Village

Knights Point
Lake Paragina
Lake Moeraki
Mount Hooker
2652m

2200m
Lake
Puka

Haast
Okuru
Haast
Haast

2499m
Mt Huxley
Lake
Ohau
Twize
Ohau

Jackson Head
Jackson Bay
Waiatoto
Jackson
Bay
Arawhata
Lake
Ellery

2149m
Mt Turner
Makarora
Young Range
Hunter

Lake Ohau
Lodge
Clearburn

Omarama
Birch Hill
1877m
Ahuriri

Cascade Point
Haast Range

1134m
Mt Theta
Mount Aspiring
National Park
3033m
Mt Aspiring

Dumar
Ote
1779

Awarua Point
Big Bay
Martins Bay
Lake
Wilmot
Olivine Range
Pyke

2446m
Climax Peak
Dart
Lochnagar
1840m
Mount
Aspiring
Maungawera

Glendhu Bay
Wanaka
Middle Peak

Lake
Wanaka
Lake
Hawea
Lake Hawea
Lindis Valley
Luggate
Tarras
Queensberry
St Bathans

Becks

Yates Point
Lake
McKerrow
2723m
Mt Tutoko
Milford
Sound
Milford
Sound
1692m
Mitre Peak
Milford
Track
Shotover

Skippers
Canyon
2245m
Mt Aurum

Cardrona
1651m
Arrowtown
Cromwell
Matakanui
Omakau

Poison Bay

Paradise
Coronet Peak
Galloway

Sutherland
Sound
Bligh Sound
1966m
Milford
Hollyford
Glenorchy
Kinloch
Lake
Gunn

Queenstown
(★Skyline Gondola)
Gibbston
Nevis
Crossing
Clyde
Alexandra

Bounty
Haven
George Sound
Barrier Peak
Cascade
Creek
Knobs Flat
1990m
Lake
Wakatipu

Fruitlands
Shingle
Creek
1889m
Lake
Roxburgh

2036m
Mt Eglinton

Mt
Nicholas
Kingston

Rocky Mount
Roxburgh

McDougall
Expedition Peak
1314m

North
Fiord
Te Anau Downs
2022m
Mt Mavora

Fairlight
1474m

Millers Fl.

Caswell Sound
Charles Sound
Nancy Sound
Thompson Sound
1484m
Double Peak
Middle Fiord
Lake
Te
Anau
North
Mavora
Lake
Jane Peak
Eyre Mountains

Park Hill
845m
Mt Wendon
Kelso

Secretary
Island
1453m
Te Anau
Waikaia

Waikaka

Doubtful Sound
1303m
Mt Forbes
Fiordland
South Fiord
The Key
Five Rivers
Cattle
Flat
Walpara
Lumsden
Mandeville
671m
Waikaka

Dagg Sound
Lake
Beattie
National
1569m
Gladstone Peak
Mossburn
Balfour
Dipton
Waimea Hill
Gol

1612m
Mt Cusack
Park
Lake
Manapouri
1615m
Blackmount
Monowai
Birchwood
Nightcaps
Pukemutu
Te Tipua
Matau

Breaksea
Island
Resolution
Island
Green
Lake
Lake
Monowai
Clifden
Woodlaw
Winton
Hedgehope
Waimumu
Waiariki

Dusky
Sound
981m
Mt Bradshaw
1722m
Cameron Mountains
Otautau
Drummond
Fairfax
Dacre
Glenham

West
Cape
Cape Providence
Chalky
Island
Coal
Island
Puysegur
Point
Tuatapere
Thornbury
Lorneville
Kennington
Gor
Roa

Te Waewae
Orepuki
Te Waewae Bay
Lake
Poteriteri
Wakapatu
Wakaputa Point
Riverton
Orepuki
Colac
Bay
Howells
Point
Greenhills
Invercargill
Awarua
Toeto

Sand Hill
Point
Centre
Island
Bluff
Tiwai
Point

Black Rock
Point
Foveaux
Strait
Ruapu
Island

980m
Mount
Anglem
Christmas Village
Bay

Codfish Island
Halfmoon Bay
East Cape
Shelter Po

Mason Bay
Stewart
Island
Stewart Island
Rakiura
National Par

Doughboy Bay
750m
Mount Allen

South Red Head Point
470m
Broad Head

Big South
Cape Island
South Cape

Clayton
Geraldine
Coldstream

Lake
Tekapo
Lake
Tekapo
Fairlie
Burkes
Pass
Opuha
Temuka
Albury
Cave
Motukaika
Timaru
1597m
Mt Nessing
Pareora

Hakataramea
Downs
Haldon
Otaio
Hunter
Wainono
Lagoon
Lake
Benmore
Waihaorunga
Waimate
Waitangi
Lake
Aviemore
Willowbridge

ata
83
Lake Waitaki
82
Hakataramea
Waitaki Valley
Tawai
Waitaki
Duntroon
Awamoko
Pukeuri

Maerewhenua
Tapui
Ngapara
Oamaru
Cape Wanbrow
Danseys
Pass
Five Forks
Mt Ida 1692m
Herbert
Maheno
Kakanui
Idaburn
1304m
Mt Dasher

Ranfurly
85
Kyeburn
Morrisons
Gimmerburn
Macraes
Flat
85
Dunback
Katiki
polburn
Hyde
87
Stoneburn
Nenthorn
710m
Shag Point
Palmerston

Poolburn
Reservoir
Paerau
Middlemarch
Taieri
Merton
Waikouaiti
Puketeraki
Taiaroa Head
Manorburn
eservoir
Greenland
Reservoir
Shannon
Mount
Allan
1132m
Waitati
Port Chalmers
Otago Peninsula
Lake
Onslow
Clarks Junction
Mosgiel
DUNEDIN
Lake
Mahinerangi
Allanton

Raes
Junction
Waipori Falls
Lawrence
Berwick
Crookston
Tuapeka
Mouth
Round Hill
Taieri Mouth
Milton
mahaka
Pukeawa
Crichton
Glenledi
Toko Mouth

Waipahi
Clinton
Kaitangata
Balclutha
araia
Waitepeka
Molyneux Bay
719m
Mt Cattins
Purekireki
Kaka Point
Nugget Point
Rosebery
Owaka
Surat Bay

Mokoreta
Catlins
Forest Park
Papatowai
Tautuku Bay
Chaslands
uarry
ills
ose
Waikawa
Chaslands Mistake
Porpoise Bay
Curio Bay
aipapa
oint
Haldane Bay

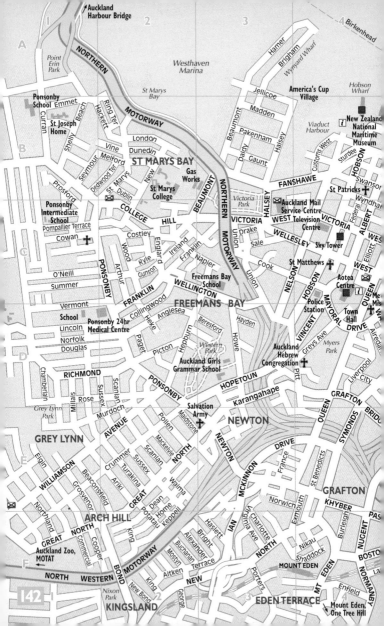